Movie Yoga
How Every Film Can Change Your Life

Tav Sparks

Hanford Mead Publishers, Inc.
Santa Cruz, California USA

Movie Yoga

Tav Sparks

Movie Yoga: How Every Film Can Change Your Life.
Copyright © 2009 by Tav Sparks. All rights reserved.

No part of this book may be reproduced, stored in a retrieval system, or transmitted, in any form or by any means, electronic, mechanical, photocopying, recording or otherwise, without the prior written permission of the publisher. For information: address Hanford Mead Publishers, Inc., P.O. Box 8051, Santa Cruz, CA 95061-8051, USA. Tel: 1.831.459.6855 Fax: 1.831.426.4474 www.hanfordmead.com

FIRST EDITION

ISBN 13: 978-1-59275-020-7   (alk. paper)

ISBN 10: 1-59275-020-6   (alk. paper)

Manufactured in the United States of America

This edition is printed on Ph neutral paper that meets the American National Standards Institute Z39.48 Standard.

Cover art by Sunny Strasberg, Fun Art Exhibits

Cover design by Daniel Cook Design, Inc.

Photo of Tav Sparks by Gordon Edwards

10 9 8 7 6 5 4 3 2 1

Library of Congress Cataloging-in-Publication Data

Sparks, Tav.
  Movie yoga : how every film can change your life / Tav Sparks. — 1st ed.
    p. cm.
  Includes index.
  ISBN 978-1-59275-020-7 (alk. paper)
  1. Motion pictures—Psychological aspects. I. Title.
  PN1995.S613 2009
  791.4301'9—dc22
                          2008048348

With Acknowledgment and Gratitude

First, to my true friends and publishers, Kylea Taylor and Jim Schofield, for their trust, inspiration, creativity, faith, and support. And to Kylea for her vision, editing, and otherwise total midwifing of our *Movie Yoga* project.

Also to Leslie Keenan, Muse, for her inspiration. To Sunny Strasburg, for conveying beauty, awe, and mystery through her cover art. Thanks to Ted Riskin, as well, for his editing and proofreading yoga.

And of course to a few of my "neighborhood" Movie Yogis: My sons, Ason and Bryn, my wife Cary, Christina and Stan Grof, Matthew Stelzner and Mark Stelzner, Kathleen and Jack Silver, Jai Uttal, Diana Medina, Nienke Merbis, Patapata Lulu, Lynda Griebenow. And to all my friends and co-workers in all the workshops and play times we've had all over the world, whom I've enticed to endure an endless procession of movies, while I indulged my twisted psyche. I hope you are not ruined forever.

And to my Mom, for the passion in her eyes on a rainy, after-school day in '57, when out of nowhere, all lit up, she turns to my sisters and me in the backseat of our Chevy wagon cruising down Mulberry Street in Macon, Georgia, and says, "I know, you wanna go see *The Wizard of Oz*?"

And finally, to the creative spirit in every filmmaker and every filmgoer in history for blessing us all with this chance to feel a deeper connection with our true selves through movies.

CONTENTS

Acknowledgments		5
Contents		7
Part I	How Movies Became a Yoga	9
Chapter 1	Get Your Ticket	11
Chapter 2	Where We Get the Back Story	17
Chapter 3	On Being Entertained	24
Chapter 4	The Game	30
(Diagram)	Awareness Positioning System™	41
Chapter 5	The Zone	46
Chapter 6	I Laughed, I Cried	52
Part II	Lights, Camera, Action!	73
Chapter 7	Getting Seated	75
Chapter 8	The Safe Zone	78
(Diagram)	Death/Rebirth Matrix	80
Chapter 9	The Trapped Zone	94
Chapter 10	The War Zone	109
Chapter 11	Death	129
Chapter 12	The Free Zone	135
Part III	The Playbook	157
Chapter 13	Been There, Done That... A Lot!	159
Chapter 14	Living in the Mystery	170
Chapter 15	Epilogue: Sunshine	178
Appendices		
Appendix A	Movies for Movie Yoga	181
Appendix B	Examples Used in *Movie Yoga*	183
Index		186
Author		192

SIDEBARS

We're going to need a bigger map	26
The new oldest new thing	28
A convenience store odyssey	31
Through the eyes of a child	43
Sitting on a whale	48
Mystery schools	50
The Death/Rebirth Matrix	50
Confessions of a Fan	54
Tears	64
Biological birth	76
How to listen to a movie	82
How to eat a movie	89
Gut checks	98
The shamanic initiation	100
Addiction and the zones	110
Looks	112
Sequels	120
The movie optimist	138
The light of earendil	173

PART I

HOW MOVIES BECAME A YOGA

GET YOUR TICKET

Morpheus to Neo: *This is your last chance. After this, there is no turning back. You take the blue pill — the story ends. You wake up in your bed and believe whatever you want to believe. You take the red pill — you stay in Wonderland, and I show you how deep the rabbit-hole goes.*

~ The Matrix

Movies have absolutely blessed my life. For me, movie theaters aren't just popcorn and M&M hide-outs. They are temples. They are altars. They are the halls of mystery. They've become the sanctuary where I go to find myself, to change, to grow. And lose myself, too, to die and be reborn. Who would have thought? One of my most intense passions, movies, has given me over and over again crystal clear glimpses of a wholeness within me, and all kinds of clues about how to make the odyssey toward that wholeness.

Let's begin with a couple of questions: First, ever dreamed of changing something about yourself that could help you be in the world in a more fulfilling way? And second, ever been turned upside down by a movie? Left the theater a different person than you were when you went in? I mean seriously moved, one way or the other: uplifted, filled with hope, energized, grossed out, devastated, transformed? When this kind of radical thing happens to us, that film, or even that scene, that line of dialogue or that piece of music, can be the key to the highway, the way we can reach that fulfillment we've been dreaming of. That's what this book is all about.

Movies can be transformational. You may already know this, but it could be true in a more profound way than you imagine. Sounds revolutionary. Except it's not that complicated. We just need to do a couple of things: Pay attention to the feelings we have in one of these overwhelming movie moments, or any kind of movie moment, for that matter. And then come up with a simple way for our feelings to transform us — to work for us, to be our allies. This book's going to show us how to do this — and a whole lot more — all while we're having a good time at the movies.

There's this practice I've been doing for years now. I call it "Movie Yoga," just to keep it short and simple. I don't mean yoga like a system of body postures. That's just one definition. I mean yoga in its broadest sense, which is any spiritual practice. The word *yoga* comes from Sanskrit and means to *yoke* or to *join together.*

So, think about it for a moment: if you had to be yoked or joined to something, what would it be? I don't know about you, but for me, feeling separate or isolated — 'unyoked' to anything — can be awful. So I need to connect up my separateness with something — an inspiration, an idea, another person or persons, maybe even the rest of humanity, the planet, or the cosmos. I just feel better, more whole, when I'm connected or yoked to something larger than myself. This is what all psychological and spiritual practices try to accomplish. Believe it or not, it's what watching movies can do too.

Here's how it has worked in my life: The bottom line is that nothing is ever the same after what are, for me, those one and only films, like *Bladerunner*, the *Lord of the Rings Trilogy*, or any of the hundreds of movies I've seen that have literally transformed me, time and time again. I keep morphing. I'm just not on freeze-frame anymore. I'm like this super-hero, or, more accurately, anti-hero franchise, where, when we get to the last frame of the last reel of the latest installment, it says "To be continued." And me, well, I'm grateful to just keep riding off into some new sunset one more time. And one of the main reasons I feel this way is because there in the dark, in front of the lit-up screen, the relentless sweep of some mystery I can't name keeps on shattering me.

Truth be told, getting connected, yoked to something bigger than our isolated selves, is happening for millions of us, everywhere, whenever we feel passion and get transported. Movies aren't the only way, either, not even for me. There's my family and my work, which I feel has been a calling. There are trees and swans and music and many other gifts. But this book is going to take this one special thing, movies, and, by demonstrating how they can change our lives, show us a way for each of us to turn everything, all that we are and do and experience, into a journey of transformation. It will let us in on a very special way to get filled with wonder and awe, to grow, to change, and to be fulfilled.

Movie Yoga can be a big help for those of us who've never had a glimpse of some kind of life blueprint — a game plan for transformation that excites us, or wonder or awe in the everyday rituals we create, like hanging out in nature, listening to music, or, of course, going to the movies. This book will give us that blueprint, a game plan, and a way to use it.

It is totally possible to get that flash of brilliance, that one and only moment, which can become a thousand one and only moments. It is possible as well to have meaningful relationships, to feel full of purpose, to be passionate, and to be able to integrate all sides of our nature, the light and the dark, without having to sacrifice or repress or feel bad about the many facets of who we are. Movie Yoga shows us how to celebrate the grand sweep of life in all of its manifestations as being part of a great mystery and wholeness that we will always be moving toward. And to watch a hellava lot of movies while we're at it.

Got Popcorn?

So, once again, how about you? Are you a movies fan? *Movie Yoga* will show you how to turn something you already love doing into something you'll love even more. Don't care much for films? What if I told you that even still, movies could change your life in a big-time, positive way? Even the ones you hate. I'm going to share with you how we can transform ourselves and have a lot of fun at the same time. It works so well, you're going to think you're cheating.

Does this sound familiar? You're feeling restless. Crossed your mind the planet's maybe going to hell in a serious hurry. So you've been working on yourself some. Well, not really, but closing in on it. How many times have we said that: we want to work on ourselves? We want to exercise more, not be so depressed, have better relationships.

And speaking of working on ourselves, ever notice how we separate work and play? When was the last time you complained, "I've got to get up in the morning and go to play." We pretty much just don't think this way. But one of the few exceptions to this I know of came from an interview I heard with Bruce Springsteen. The interviewer was asking him about the early days, and did he have any other jobs besides music. And Bruce said something about not digging work. He added, "That's why they call it *playing* music."

Take movies. Almost all of us who go to movies — and that's a lot of people — go because it's fun. It's play. All except critics. That's their job. But most of them are probably like Bruce. They've picked out a gig that really floats their boat. They get paid for doing something they have a passion for.

Ever heard that line Joseph Campbell made famous, "Follow your bliss"? He was definitely tapped in. Only one small problem: Bliss is seriously elusive. I have a clue he means doing what really turns us on. But somehow I'm still missing something. If I've never experienced it, or don't even have a clear picture of what it is, like, if I have nothing to go on, how exactly am I going to follow it? I mean, all kinds of spiritual traditions will say: if we work on ourselves a lot, then we'll experience bliss. So, if that's so, then why aren't we pouring out of the office, or wherever, in droves, coming out of our uniforms, putting on some orange robes, and taking up the old begging bowl? Well for one thing, that'd be a whole lot of work.

But look at it another way. I read a book a few years ago by a director, Robert Rodriguez, called *Rebel without a Crew*. The book came out after he blew Hollywood away with his great first movie *El Mariachi*, which he did for about seven thousand dollars. His book was about how he made that film. I got all fired up and started writing screenplays. I wanted to play too, figured the best way to see the kind of movies I loved was to write them myself. Then, maybe, in some alternate universe, they'd hire me to direct my masterpieces. Anyway... But what really inspired me was when he said, "Follow your passion."

Now this really works a lot better for me, because I can relate way more to passion than I can to bliss. Passion's about feeling intensely. Not just about sex. That too, but about anything. I thought, now I'm starting to relate. If there's one thing I've done all my life, it has been to feel some real passion. Bliss? Well, how am I going to know? Is it feeling great? I mean, off-the-charts great? Or is it actually way past feeling even that, like another universe altogether? Or, hold up a tic. Could bliss be this alchemical mix of feeling good and feeling bad? Like some mysterious power emerges out of heaven and hell and takes us to a new realm totally? See what I mean about elusive?

Okay, so getting back to working on ourselves, like going to therapy, or doing yoga, or meditation, or whatever. There it is again: working on ourselves. That right there says a lot about how we feel about personal growth and transformation. I mean, these days, most of us want to change, at least a little bit. And a lot of us want to change in some kind of radical way.

But how many of us can actually say we have a true passion for transforming ourselves? For most of us, no matter what we do for personal growth, it still feels like work. And truth be told, we'd rather sit on the couch, doing whatever, as long as it doesn't feel like work. Right? Like watching a movie. Most of the time, we'd rather be entertained than have to participate. We have to have our backs right up against the wall to actually entertain the notion of getting up off that couch.

Well, what if we don't have to — get off the couch, I mean? Or maybe get off the couch sometime, but just to cruise down to the local multiplex once in a while for a change of scenery. What if we could be killing two birds — no, wait a minute, let me rephrase that. I'd better use an expression my son Bryn, who is way into nothing bad happening to animals, came up with: "What if we could pet two cats with one hand?"

Sure, watching a movie is fun, play, chillin', relaxation, being off the clock, passing some time, escaping, disappearing, fantasizing, whatever. But we would pretty much never think that going to the movies could actually be therapeutic, might actually be a powerful tool for transformation. Except it is, or can be, if we know how to do it. That's what this book is all about. We could even call it "Couch Potato Therapy".

The fun part is a no-brainer. But most of us have other motivations at play when we watch a film, even if we don't know it consciously. Movies strike chords in us. They move us, down deep. How and why this happens is something we're going to spend a lot of time on. Let's just say for now that experiences — our feelings, struggles, longings, desires, and so on — seem to be universal. Everybody goes through them. So, when it's happening to a character up on the screen, it can tap into that place where we know deep down what they're going through. We know it from the inside out, because we've felt it too.

One problem though: most of the time, a film's collaborators — the writer, director, cinematographer, soundtrack composer, and so on — create a work that exists within what I call a really narrow bandwidth of consciousness. By band-width of consciousness I mean what's important to us, what values we have. Or what our understanding or philosophy of life is. You know, like *get some money, make me happy; lose my boyfriend, make me sad; the most important thing in life is looking good; bash his head in, make me alpha dog; or fart jokes funny*, that kind of thing.

But every once in a while, the canvas is huge. For example: *Freedom, love, and truth are worth fighting for. The goal of life is to know ourselves. Or, life is an archetypal struggle between great opposing forces, like good and evil.* These are the ones that strike us so deeply that we can have a life-changing experience when we see them on the screen. Here's where it's really possible to see what I mean when I say film is a spiritual technology. It's pretty easy to get inspired by films like these.

But I would like to take it one step further. A movie doesn't have to be brilliant to move us. Nor does it have to have the broadest bandwidth to be transformational. Not in Movie Yoga it doesn't. We're going to explore a way to make every movie we could ever see be a source for changing our lives in a meaningful way. How many hours did you spend watching movies last year, either at the theater or in your living room? How many hours did you spend meditating, dancing, doing yoga, or going to therapy? Want to double your self-discovery time without breaking too much of a sweat? Yeah? Well, me too.

So, imagine we're in *The Fellowship of the Ring*, and we're a ring-bearer, and we're about to head out to Mordor to take the ring to Mount Doom. And like the hobbit, Pippin, we convince Elrond, the elf-lord of Rivendel, that the fellowship needs us on "this sort of quest." So we summon the courage to volunteer. But then as an after-thought, we also pipe up, like Pippin did, and ask, "So, where are we going?" Yeah, and what's more, how are we going to get there?

Let's just say right now that we're going to treat this whole thing, this Movie Yoga, as a game we can play. And like any game, it's got a few simple guidelines. So let's take a look — no, hang on, here's the part where the scene gets wavy and we have a fade out, and we know there's going to be some kind of back story. So, to do a riff on what Robert Rodriguez suggested in *Rebel without a Crew*, I'm going to ask you to follow my passion for a few moments. Then we're going to follow yours. Learn some Movie Yoga. Then all we have to do is play. Notice I didn't say "work"?

CHAPTER 2
WHERE WE GET THE BACK STORY

"I've seen things you people wouldn't believe: Attack ships on fire off the shoulder of Orion. I've watched C-Beams glitter in the dark near the Tan Hauser Gate. All those moments will be lost in time — like tears in the rain. Time to die.

~ Roy Battie, Nexus Six Replicant, to Deckard, the bladerunner, in *Bladerunner*

There's one of those old movie houses near where we — my partner, Cary, our son, Bryn, and I, oh, and Thunder the cat — live. It's not so old-fashioned as to be a classic — basically just seedy and cheap. You could catch new movies maybe a half-year late at half the price, if that's how you rolled. I say "you," because I never went there. I mean, I'm a snob. But not the kind of snob you're thinking, like the "I-don't-want-to-get-caught-dead-in-a-dump-like-this" kind of snob.

I'm more the "Why would anybody go see a movie with a soundtrack you'd have to strain yourself leaning forward to hear out of two tiny, tinny, static-filled speakers on either side of a smoke-smudged screen the size of a postage stamp cratered with the remains of four decades of Friday night junk food fights glistening like an oil slick in the glare of a pre-Viet Nam war era rattle-trap projector which makes way more noise than what might be happening in the movie, if you could but see or hear it?" kind of snob.

But then I saw in the paper where they fixed it up a little — put in some stadium seating and some rocking chairs. But that's not what caught my eye. It was the DLP. That stands for digital light processing, whatever that is. Think of it as a sort of a poor person's plasma. I'm not dissing it. I have a big DLP television myself and love it. What's important here, though, is that they put in digital sound and digital picture, in this funky old neighborhood place, in a kind of diamond-in-the-roughish sort of way.

Okay, that's different. Sounds like worth a try, especially since the county in Northern California where I live — supposedly one of these "meccas" of artistic sophistication — would not quite be the celestial movie theater heaven I'd hope to be sent to upon my demise as an obsessive theater critic here on planet Earth.

So Cary and I and two close friends, another movie freak couple, saw a forgettable film there, just checking things out. Impressive. A sharp digital picture and clear, pretty big sound, good bass — could have been louder. But, here's an axiom to live by, from someone who's been getting off on head-shattering rock and roll his whole life, whose job includes, among other things, listening to drumming at mega-decibel levels for hours almost every day, and who needs to feel, not hear, the movie bass track in a manner that simulates, if not a heart attack, then at least a 7.0 Richter Scale quake in his chest, and the axiom is this: the sound can always, always, be louder. But, all in all, it was worth a return.

Which was what Cary and I did, on what was for me basically a holy occasion: the re-release of *Bladerunner*, Ridley Scott's masterpiece of sci-fi noir that shattered — whoa, wait:

FLASHBACK — INT. MOVIE THEATER, MACON, GEORGIA, 1982, NIGHT

I'm three years clean from a murderous addiction. I'm with my current girlfriend, who's also in the Program. She's from Jackson, Mississippi. We're in this ratty theater, waiting on the lights to go down. We can't make up our minds whether to hit a 12 Step meeting first, maybe blow off the flick, or make the movie, then a meeting later. Besides which, we don't know one thing about the movie, *Bladerunner*, except I saw the not-too-flashy ad; it's got Hans Solo, I mean Harrison Ford, and no endorsements. So we decide on the movie.

The lights go down. There's maybe a preview or two, I don't remember. Then it's movie time. I'm not focused much on the screen. I'm more kind of all in love, leaning sideways in my seat. You know. Fresh love, fresh recovery, a heady brew. The white letters come out of a black background. Not useless information. All you need to tell you you're in the right theater. Which might not seem relevant here, except it is, because, already by this time I'm not so sure about anything.

The soundtrack: a weird electronic effect, mysterious, which twenty-five years later is as familiar as early-morning birdsong: kind of electronic, maybe a computer. Why was I not so sure back then? Because computers weren't uber-ubiquitous in that Dark Age. And then more white words scroll down — the set-up — something about androids called replicants, about replicant bounty hunters called "Bladerunners," and about when they kill a replicant it's called retirement. Hmmm... okay, wait a minute. This is, let's see, intriguing?

And then it happens. A rumble, half way between cannon fire and thunder — probably drums, a synthesizer. The words, "Los Angeles, 2019." And the best score Vangelis ever wrote blossoms out of the first image: nighttime LA through fog/smog, diffused light, and fire-bursts from nameless industrial processors. A flying car jets out of the background coming right at us in the seats, then on by, and another flies out of the foreground, heading across the nightmare skyline.

I'm gone, baby, gone. And, after all these years, I'm not back yet. Because I am transported into another world. I am taken from myself. And who I am a minute before doesn't exist anymore, because the music and the images blow me apart, like a great rip in the fabric of what I think reality is. And I am discovering that same old thing that Hamlet told his best friend after seeing his father's ghost: "There are more things in heaven and earth, Horatio, than are dreamt of in your philosophy." You better believe it.

Here in the theater, I am like the Fool in the tarot deck, big major arcana card Number Zero, fluting around, dancing off some cliff. I have no clue, not even a whiff of awareness, that I am just plain caught in my own picture, sleep-walking, like I know I'm doing it, young lover-high, all cleaned up and recovery-ready; got the world by the whatever you want.

And then I'm teleported through that jagged, velvet rip, like Colonel Kurtz says near the end of *Apocalypse Now*, when he's laying it out for Captain Willard who's taken the path up-river into madness to find himself in the heart of darkness, "Like a snail crawling along a straight razor." That's how sharp and exquisite it is to lose myself, to let go — no, to be let go of into a new reality, a new self.

That's what Ridley Scott did, and the writers, Hampton Fancher and David Peoples, and the special effects avatar, Doug Trumbull, and Vangelis, the music god, and the cinematographer Jordan Cronenweth, way before Industrial Light and Magic. But this is industrial, and it is light and magic. Some profound, alien orchestra of image and sound, like these guys are the engines of creation, Brahman himself thinking up the heavens, while the Great Mother labors to birth the whole trip: movies, the fruit of her womb. That's what this crew tapped, these Hollywood players who made *Bladerunner*. That's what they all tap: cosmic forces of creation.

And we the Fools get to dance off the cliff into the arms of other worlds, and, better yet, come back: never-the-same, star-eyed, and full of wonder at the mystery, seeing the world with new eyes, walking it with new feet, feeling with finer emotions, and letting the exquisite intensity of being a new-born begin to inform who we are and how we're going to walk out of this darkened temple when the lights go up and say, "This is a new bright night." That's what *Bladerunner* does to me that first time. It wasn't the first movie to do it either, and it won't be the last. But let me tell you: this is church.

BACK TO SCENE:

The present again, or at least the present where we were in the story a minute ago: Cary and I at the re-re-release. So I've seen *Bladerunner* maybe fifty times or more, in several different incarnations, at home and in the theaters. It's one of the only films in the past few decades that gets a theater run every decade or two. This latest time is because Ridley Scott says he's got the definitive cut: all digital sound and image, some things we've never seen before. So you know I'm there. I'm there like it's the pilgrimage to Mecca, like it's Kumbha Mela, and here I am with one-hundred million other devotees coming together, again. Going to gather at the Ganges one more time.

So the river of this incarnation is the neighborhood grind house with DLP and rocking chairs and the '70s concession stand and a little bitty bathroom. And it's like that first time on the south side of Macon. No it's not. Because I didn't know what was coming then. Okay, I don't know what's coming this time either. What I'm saying is, even though I didn't know then and I don't know now, what I don't know both times is different. And you may think I'm talking in riddles, but I'm not. This has meaning.

It says something about the power of movies in my life. But it says more than that. It's about what it means to live in the mystery as much as possible every minute. So that way, each moment, even if you think maybe you've done this thing before, you have the opportunity to get blown away every time, and blown away again. And it's this capacity that makes me grateful I'm doing this Earth trip, to be able to get rocked over and over, by whatever, by anything, it doesn't matter — by every moment, so that the world is filled with mystery and the threat of death.

Don't let this scare you. I don't just mean physical death. I'm talking about the possibility of the demise of a little false self I have some serious investment in. About that part of me ceasing to exist from one moment to the next. About the person I think I am, the one I'm getting all familiar with, and truth be told, a little tired of. About the one that keeps me restless and moving and looking toward the next sunrise, like maybe what I'm dreaming of is just about to shine down all over me, a newborn self. Believe it or not, we can actually live poised for the next death, the next moment that rearranges everything; make a spiritual practice out of it, a *yoga*, as they say.

So, here I am one more time, thinking I know what this trip's all about: relationship, those kinds of things, how to negotiate the shoals through these troubled waters known as life on planet earth. And I think I know what *Bladerunner*'s all about? Well, that first hit of deep, dark, digital black, and the bloom of Vangelis' score on the screen coming through those not too shabby speakers I was talking about, are like vast tectonic plates of beauty shifting in the core of my soul, and I'm weeping. I'm home, once again. I'm in that zone. I know it. And I don't.

Like the drop-ship pilot says as she radios the mother ship while she takes Ripley and the marines to big bad monster death down on the terra-formed planet in James Cameron's *Aliens*: I am "in the pike, five by five." Like the Nexus Six replicant Roy Battie's soliloquy at the end of *Bladerunner*, "I've seen things you people wouldn't believe."

I see details in the background, actual characters I never knew were there. Lines of dialogue I've never heard. And this is not to mention what Scott changed and added. This is just what the digital copy did. There are no words. Like the Jodie Foster character in Robert Zemekus' *Contact* remarks after she bursts through a series of wormholes in the dimension-crossing machine the aliens give Earth the blueprint for, and she's standing on a beach in a new world, looking at two suns: "I had no idea. They should have sent a poet."

You know, that's right. Because no idea, nothing from that part of the brain is going to explain the kinds of experiences we have that really change us. Because an experience is beyond that part of the mind, and the closest we can get with words is probably poetry. What I'm saying is that life can be filled with these kinds of opportunities, where we'd have to be a poet to share it with others in any meaningful kind of way.

But for me it happens in movies. And you know what? That puts me in the company, now and then, of ecstatics. Lets me hang with, every once in a while, some kind of tribe of pop culture dervishes. Nothing special, because like I said, we all do it in our own ways, or want to. We just have to get our socks knocked off once or twice by something, and then pay attention. Like, "what the hell is that?"

And when we get a hit of what's making heaven be knock knock knocking at our door, I believe we have a good chance to go about creating something special for ourselves. We start, sometimes accidentally, putting ourselves in situations where that kind of magic might happen again. That's what I mean by making a yoga, making a practice, out of that thing. It's what I'm doing with movies. I'm showing up for Movie Yoga. And that's what this book is all about: how to take the thread of something that has the power to change us and weave it all through the tapestry of who each of us is.

Every once in a while, if we're lucky, or have grace — however you want to look at it — we might get rocked so hard that our world falls apart. It's in those times we may get a glimpse of a blueprint, of some whole self we might be becoming. Sometimes it's just a feeling. Other times, it can be like a tidal wave that takes us, body and soul. *Bladerunner* nights, or whatever kind of movie nights yours are, throw a diamond sharp spotlight on that blueprint I've had a glimpse of it now and then. And maybe even a piece of the plan of how I'm going to get there.

I feel like Frodo from *The Lord of the Rings*, the books that inspired so many of us, way back in my elitist prep school days. These are the books, of course, that Peter Jackson has paid such incredible homage to decades later, in the greatest films I've ever seen. Like Frodo and millions of others today, I've become a ring bearer, and I'm off on an epic adventure without the slightest clue of what I'm up against.

But, you know what? No worries. Because I got all kinds of yellow brick roads out there, and just about all of them will take me to a movie. Then I just take a seat. Let the lights go down. Open my eyes, look up at the magic screen, where if I'm even just half awake, my life will be reeling out there in front of me frame by frame.

All I have to do is pay attention. Let that story do its dance upon my soul, read the tracings of the dance like a swan's flight across the setting moon on a still winter dawn. And, when I walk out of there, I am not the same person I was when I went in. I'm just a little more connected up, with life, with humanity, with the Whole Thing, in some fresh, surprising way. A way that keeps me full of awe and wonder at how little I actually know. And full of a passion to embrace the world with a new heart, and with one eye on the next yellow brick road.

ON BEING ENTERTAINED

Jack: *What are your legs?*
Archie Hamilton: *Steel springs.*
Jack: *What are they gonna do?*
Archie Hamilton: *Hurl me down the track.*
Jack: *How fast can you run?*
Archie Hamilton: *As fast as a leopard.*
Jack: *How fast are you gonna run?*
Archie Hamilton: *As fast as a leopard.*
Jack: *Right, then let's see you do it.*

~ *Gallipoli*

Okay, so this may seem a little weird, that transformation can happen when you are having your cake and eating it too. But even though such an idea may seem kind of blasphemous, it doesn't have to be. Most early cultures didn't really have entertainment the way we do now. A couple of millennia ago, art and theater were participatory. Their purpose was for the growth of the individual, but more importantly, transformation of the community. It was about ritual celebration, a way of moving closer to the Great Mystery. You didn't just sit back and let something happen to someone else while you watched. You were a part of it. Everybody got down together.

Maximus, played by Russell Crowe in Ridley Scott's *Gladiator*, was a noble, heart-broken warrior seeking revenge for the murder of his family. Do you remember the scene in the arena, after he annihilated about ten A-list mega-gladiators, and he's pretty much disgusted? So he looks up at the masses crowded into the stadium, who might as well have been at the movies. And just after he throws his bloody sword at them, he says, "Are you not entertained?" Well, he was onto something.

Aristotle, way before even the fictional Maximus, pretty much nailed it. He said that the purpose of viewing a play, whether tragedy or comedy, but particularly tragedy, was something called *catharsis*. In order to experience catharsis, the audience has to participate in the play. They're not there just to be entertained. And the way they participate is by having an experience of identification with the hero or other characters in the play. Same thing with a movie.

So, with tragedy, we have a hero, who has a tragic flaw that screws him up and causes his downfall. And the audience, then, would identify with what the hero goes through. In other words, they would get activated emotionally, psychologically, and spiritually. They would feel with the hero, feel his or her sadness, despair, loss, or whatever he or she went through.

Now, for those of us interested in Movie Yoga, this is important. It's not that the audience was just observing the pain of the hero or the other characters. They would actually feel their own emotions within themselves. They would discover that all the grand emotions people go through — hate, love, envy, anger, joy, sorrow, and so on — have a universal or common ground. We all feel them. They're each ours, but everybody else's too.

So, if we were in Athens, let's say, watching a play, or we're in our home town, out at the flicks with a friend, and we identified with the emotions of the hero or some other character going through all that he or she does, then we would have what Aristotle called a catharsis. And that, right there, is the starting point of Movie Yoga. This isn't a fad, the latest snake oil gimmick. This game's got one serious pedigree.

Okay, why is catharsis, or going through all these feelings, a big deal? It's a big deal because catharsis is healing. It's cleansing. It's a way we empty ourselves of the dammed-up reservoir of emotions that can eat at us for our whole lives. Just about any type of psychological or spiritual practice has a component of getting in touch with feelings. But it's not just emotions that can get freed up. Our bodies can too. And even the way we think can get turned upside down. It can be as radical as seeing the whole world differently. And it can be as life-changing as feeling as though a part of us has died, and another part has been reborn.

This is what people go to therapy for, even if they don't realize it when they start. It's one of the reasons we meditate. It's one of the reasons we work on ourselves. It's how we get free. And, here's what we're getting at: it can be the main reason we watch films. Catharsis. Maybe what Maximus was so enraged about was why the audience was there in the first place. Maybe what he was driving at was, "Why aren't *you* in the arena? It ain't working unless you can feel what I feel."

We're Going to Need a Bigger Map

I couldn't imagine what all the fuss was about when Jaws *first came out, until I saw it. Then I got it. It was like this incredible modern Moby Dick tale, especially the final act, when they're out on the water. The whole last part of* Moby Dick *was the final chase for the white whale, Moby Dick, with chapter titles like "The Chase," "The First Day," "The Second Day," and so on. Herman Melville's classic novel had been amazing up to this point. But here, in the chase, was where it took off for me and really moved into epic territory. And that's what happened in this final stage of* Jaws: *the epic hunt for the shark. "We're going to need a bigger boat." How cool was that?*

Whenever we enter epic territory, like with Jaws, *we're going to have to open to, and find words for, the psycho-spiritual death/rebirth experience I've been referring to so far in some of my past movie adventures. Death and rebirth has been the metaphor, the framework, for how I experience transformation through a movie. I've been imprinted since my first movie breakthrough. It's the path I know the deepest. I can think back over the hundreds of movies I've experienced, looking through this lens of death and rebirth. And what's amazing is that almost all of them seem to be at least partly, even if unconsciously, created with some aspect of the death/rebirth process as a major theme. And, in many of them, death/rebirth is so obvious, the filmmakers just had to be doing it on purpose.*

The simplest way to describe death/rebirth is that it just means some part of ourselves ends. Some way we have of operating in the world, thinking or feeling about ourselves — other people, the world, or the cosmos, how we identify ourselves, or who we think we are — is finished. And then a new way takes its place.

Sometimes the change is minor, pretty smooth to go through. We don't have much investment in the old way, so the new one comes pretty easily. But sometimes it's tougher. Most of us sort of like at least something about who we

are. Maybe you thought you were kinda good looking in high school. But when you got to college, it felt like the big leagues by comparison, and you weren't such a knock-out any more. So you had to die to this self-image. This may have caused you some trouble, but not too much. It didn't kill you. You got over it.

Or else it can hurt like hell, because the old self-image might be all we know. All our self-esteem is wrapped up in this one identity. And to give it up, without knowing what's going to take its place, terrifies us. Let's say you see yourself as the hottest lover between two sheets. And you really have serious energy around this image. Like Christian from the TV series Nip/Tuck, who had a rough childhood filled with neglect and abuse. So, one of the ways he unconsciously tries to make up for this is through sexual conquests, which he engages in without actually giving up any part of his vulnerable or wounded self.

But something comes along, like a baby, which is what happens to him, and all of a sudden he's confronted with all his childhood aloneness, abuse, and low self-esteem. This is when the change assumes epic proportions and can literally feel like a death. We may fight this kind of death for years, hanging on for dear life, scratching and clawing for all we're worth. Because that's what feels at stake: all we think we're worth.

The new identity that emerges after the death of the old identity always helps us be in the world in a more fulfilling way. I'm not saying it doesn't hurt. It does, but the pain has meaning. It'll have a purpose. Lots more on death/rebirth later, because it's a foundation of this whole Movie Yoga trip.

The Dream Factory

Movies absolutely permeate our culture. Hollywood, every country's 'Hollywood', is a dream factory. Even if a lot of what they put out may sometimes feel inconsequential, it's still a spiritual technology. The possibility is always there to create a masterpiece, a work of art. In one sense, movies are a product of the culture from which they spring. But in another way, movies have helped shape world culture in lasting ways.

I'll never forget the first *Star Wars*. No way millions of others will either. I wasn't one of those who saw it as a child, for whom it would shape the way they see the world forever. No, for me those childhood imprints were from other films. Films like *Twenty Thousand Leagues Under the Sea, Bambi, Old Yeller, Captain's Courageous, The Wizard of Oz, The Seventh Voyage of Sinbad,*

Rodan, Bridge on the River Kwai, Ben Hur, Taris Bulbar, Davy Crockett, and *Gone with the Wind.* And yes, *The Mummy, The Blood of Dracula, I Was a Teenage Frankenstein,* and, truth be told, *Psycho.* The list goes on and on.

I was twenty-seven when *Star Wars* came out, seven years after *Fantasia,* the first major death/rebirth I ever had, and I'll go into detail about that later. When I saw *Star Wars,* I was well on the way down my epic, spiritual path. Of course I loved the space opera aspect to it, the swashbuckling adventure and romance. But what really blew my mind was the Force. Finally, in modern popular culture, in a way that was accessible to billions, was a deep spiritual principle. World religions could be spending another five millennia before that many people all over were introduced to such a radical concept, much less taken it as so unthreatening, yet easy-to-use, as in, "May the Force be with you." Not to mention the in-your-face recognition of the struggle between the Light and the Dark Side.

And back to *Jaws,* the first great blockbuster. It so viciously tapped an archetypal fear in humans. On the surface — well, not exactly on the surface, as we all know, but way down deep — there's our fear of sharks. But what really got people about it? What about the great unknown, the Mystery inside us? And I'm not talking about the over-worked Freudian id thing. I'm talking about some mythic Pandora's box: more like the vast collective unconscious that Carl Jung wrote about.

The New Oldest New Thing

In one sense, thinking in terms of death/rebirth is a new and radical way of being in the world. But really it's the most ancient natural process on the planet. We might feel it if we slow down in any meaningful way, take a time-out for any period, through therapy, retreat, time in nature, meditation, whatever. Or even if we don't, life can bring us to a screeching halt in the thousand ways it can: accident, illness, loss, the death of someone close. It's always possible to feel this cycle, the total rightness of it, deep inside. There it will be: rising up like a cool, refreshing mist from down under the great linear struggles and cravings we all go through.

It can feel like an absolute miracle when, at some magical point during our lives, the death/rebirth cycle bursts into the light of our awareness, like it did that time for me in the theater watching Bladerunner *and during a whole lot of other movies. Spontaneously, unlooked for, unasked for; yet there it is.*

Suddenly everything is different, even though everything's still the same. After we give up all our struggles to hang on to whoever we thought we were before, there's nothing left to do but let go, and just say, "Welcome."

We may have hurt like hell. It could have felt like dying. But in the end, after the death, when the rebirth comes, it can be the most beautiful thing we've ever imagined. You know that gospel tune, "Amazing Grace"? "How sweet the sound." I'm not kidding. When some cherished part of ourselves dies, when we surrender, let go, finally, after fighting to stay the way we were (even though it might have made us miserable), some part of us is pretty certain it wasn't caused by us being some kind of hero, or anybody special. Turns out it's a gift, plain and simple.

Just about everybody who's attempting some kind of self-discovery is diving beneath the surface of his or her psyche, many just splashing around near the surface waters a little bit, but others diving way down deep. And you know what? It's not all sharks and nameless monsters down there either, even if that's what we're afraid of most. No, there are dolphins and mermaids and things more beautiful than we can even imagine.

So what if you forget seventy-five percent of the movies you see before you get to the parking lot. I've never met one single person who doesn't have at least some kind of powerful memory from some scene in some film. Not one. Is a single memory enough? You bet it is. It takes no more than one powerful experience to change our lives, one way or the other. Right? You know I am. Take a look back. Not too hard, is it? Memories, one way or the other. Try to remember one movie that stands out for you, for better or for worse. Easier than you thought, isn't it?

I have a mentor, Angeles Arrien, who says that any dream we can remember is strong medicine. To honor her, we might even take it a bit further: Any memory we have at all is strong medicine. And then we could piggy-back on that and take it just a little deeper still: Any movie we can remember is right up there with dreams. It's definitely strong medicine. We remember it for a reason. Our job, if we want to do this yoga, this practice, is to wake up. Something really meaningful is sitting right there inside us going, "Hello, pay attention. No accident you keep feeling me." Want to find out why? Right, then let's see you do it.

THE GAME

Tyler Durden: *We were raised on television to believe we'd all be millionaires, movie gods, rock stars, but we won't. And we're starting to figure that out.*

~ Fight Club

Thetis: *What if courage and imagination became everyday mortal qualities?*

~ Clash of the Titans

One Stab: *Some people hear their own inner voices with great clearness and they live by what they hear. Such people become crazy, but they become legends.*

~ Legends of the Fall

In Which We Learn How the Game Got Started

Remember that job I have that I said feels like a calling? Well, Cary and I and many of my friends conduct workshops for seekers. Although it's not the main focus, we show a lot of films at these, for two reasons. First (and I'm sure this will come as a shock to you) I'm addicted to movies. So, along with all the other practices we do, we're going to see some movies, that's all there is to it.

Second (and to be honest this is the main reason), movies just seem to put everything the workshop participants are going through in a new light that really supports their experience and integration. Watch a film, have an experience of the things we are trying to communicate, get the visuals, the music, let it pour through not just our minds, but our bodies and our emotions too, and instead of just thinking about it, we really get it.

So over the years, the films I show at our workshops have become a bit notorious. Participants either think I'm tapped in, or they doubt my sanity. I've shown dozens of different movies, from obscure masterpieces like the Spanish film, *Cabeza de Vaca,* by Nicolas Echevarria, to classics like Sidney Lumet's *Equus.* I've even based an entire training week on Peter Jackson's astounding *Lord of the Rings* trilogy.

One thing I believe with all my heart: films are not going to give us something we don't already have in some form within us. All they do is trigger whatever is already there, so that it can come up into our awareness. And when that happens, we heal emotionally, psychologically, and spiritually. This ability of films to trigger us is hugely important, and we'll amplify it considerably when we focus on the actual directions of how to play the Movie Yoga game.

Most participants really get off on the experience. And even those who find the movies challenging are pretty down with the fact that the shows are bringing into their awareness something relevant. They also understand that they're healing from seeing the film clips, provided they're willing to use some simple guidelines. This is what the rest of this book will be about: we can watch movies, and by paying attention to our reactions to them, we can actually go through meaningful transformative experiences with lasting benefits.

A Convenience Store Odyssey

You can go through a death/rebirth just easing down to the corner market to get a soda. Know what I mean? You feel like you're dying of thirst, so you're on maximum overdrive, obsessing on that first crisp taste. But you just about flatten somebody on a bike, so you slam on the brakes. And this causes you to catch a yellow light. So, then you're stuck for what feels like eternity at the red light — you're freaking, energy's building up like a volcano about to erupt. Finally you're freed up to go.

Soon — actually it's just soon in real clock time, because inside you it's more like a six-pack of ice ages — you reach the store door, but what looks like a rabid dog growls at you. Except he's more like a fire-breathing dragon by now. Yet somehow you make it past the guardian of the temple and stagger inside. But — no way — they're out of your brand. No, wait — there's one. Just let me — you left your wallet at home. And now it's not a soda, it's life

and death, and all the forces of the universe are arrayed on the battlefield. And — you get the picture. DEATH, baby! Utterly defeated, you sleep-walk out the door to face the dark universe without your life-elixir. Only to trip over six cases of the very beverage which the goddess of gifts just delivered in her chariot, I mean truck. You fall to your knees, hear a jingle in your pocket, and lo and behold, you got change! REBIRTH! Nothing but a soda, right?

Truth be told, death/rebirth is the natural way of being on the planet. But what makes all this seem so unnatural to us is that we (and our parents and their parents' and grandparents before them) have been taught since we were born to live and think in a totally opposite way from death/rebirth cycles. We've grown up believing that the only change worth making is to keep getting better, richer, bigger, smarter, prettier, faster, cooler — forever. In our culture, change is all linear — a one way trip. More is better. If I can just make a few more dollars. If we can just process a few more billion barrels of oil, cut down a few more trees, acquire just a little more real estate. Get the picture?

Everybody trying to get fulfilled at the expense of everybody else. And meanwhile Mother Nature just sweeps along going through her cycles — day goes to night and night to day. The seasons change. Everything gets born, and dies. Life continues in new forms. But we, the humans, are the only critters on the planet who think that cycles are for sissies. That if we have a down cycle — where we fall back, have to regroup, lay low, rethink, or whatever — it's because we're weak, or something's wrong — not because it's the natural and inevitable way things always grow and change.

How to Play with This Book

My younger son Bryn is one of those adventurers who throws directions out the window. PlayStation 3, X-Box 360 — it doesn't matter. Actually he takes after my older son Ason, who's been known to throw a whole lot of directions out the window over the years too. Oh, and by the way, both these gentlemen are deadly serious Movie Yogis, with whom I've had many unforgettable theater adventures down through the years.

But when Bryn gets a game, he's in it. When he gets to a new level, he doesn't even stop to learn what the new objective is. He just forges ahead into the unknown. For him, this is where the juice is — the excitement, the fun. Every once in a while, if he gets stuck too badly, he'll look back at the directions or the strategy guide. His trip is, "Let's get on with it already!" Come to think of it, sounds kinda like a genetic family trait.

The Game

You may be feeling the same way about Movie Yoga. You're fired up, ready for some movie-watching — maybe even some transformation. You're going, as they say in the Coen brothers' *Miller's Crossing*, "So, what's the rumpus? Where's the part where we do some dying and getting reborn?" Somebody else says, "No kidding. I've been in therapy for years. I already meditate every day. I don't need any more psycho-babble. I know how to work on myself. I want to play."

If either of these is you, sounds like you're primed for the game. You won't need to read the next couple of chapters right now. You can skip ahead and dive right in. Still, you may find later that these chapters are worthwhile too. Just like Bryn, if you get stuck in some level, you can always consult the Awareness Positioning System™ (APS) – described in the next couple of chapters — for a pointer here and there. What I'll do here is give you a stripped down, bare bones paragraph of what Movie Yoga is — Movie Yoga for the Fast Lane. Read that. If you want just a little more structure, turn to page 35 for "Game Guidelines — The Short Form". Then, all you have to do is play.

In the Appendices, you'll find two lists. The first is a complete index of every movie mentioned in the book. The second lists all the movies used in the book as examples of certain levels of the Death/Rebirth Matrix, which is the primary map of transformation we'll be using to play the game. In addition, all movie titles appear in the Index in italics with page references.

Thumbing through the text, you probably already noticed that there are sections here and there, marked by a film strip, that are just me musing along, giving some supplemental facts and observations about using movies as a spiritual practice. You can read these, or not, at any time, as the mood grabs you. Or as you get some kind of interesting insight while you're playing the game. What may seem irrelevant on the first run-through might jump out at you later on.

But if you decide to skip these 'film-strip sections', no problem. There's nothing in them that you absolutely have to have in order to play. This goes, too, for those of you who like to follow the directions before you attempt to put something together or break in a new electronic toy. For all of you, remember: The film strip sections are there if you're looking for something more at any point.

So now, if you're like Ason and Bryn, and want to skip most of the directions, head on over to the Chapter, "I Laughed, I Cried," starting on page 52, or to the Death chapter starting on page 129. In the latter, be looking for the heading, "Test Screening." It might also help to read about the Awareness

Positioning System™ (APS), on page 38 (chart on page 41) and the Death/Rebirth Matrix Chart on page 80. These are where I go the deepest into movies. So, now, here is lean, mean Movie Yoga. Good playing!

Movie Yoga for the Fast Lane

We sit on our sofa, or in a movie theater. We watch a movie and pay attention to our reactions to it. Instead of crediting the film for what we're feeling, we look inside ourselves. We try to find what it is within us that has been triggered by the scene in the movie. It may be something we've known really well all our lives, or it might be something brand new – marvelous, or mystifying, or both.

Whatever it is, once we trace the feeling, as deep as we are able, we allow it to emerge into our awareness, and we embrace it as much as we can. That's it. What we're actually doing while eating chocolate and popcorn, while sitting on our sofa or in the theater, is engaging in one of the deepest psychological and spiritual practices known to humanity. And we thought we were just having fun.

The Least Dangerous Game

For you on-the-fencers, a quick word about games in general: Here's something that Alonzo, the Denzel Washington character, told Hoyt, played by Ethan Hawke, in *Training Day,* the relentlessly entertaining character study from Antoine Fuqua. He was trying to rationalize all the tricky and devious crap he was pulling in the streets. So he said to Hoyt, "The game's chess; it ain't checkers."

Yeah, it's a board game. It has pieces you move around. But way different rules and moves. A whole other universe, entirely. It doesn't make sense to sit down at a chess board and get all unnerved because it's not checkers. Doesn't mean we don't do it sometimes, but it's a waste of energy. Just get up and go find some checkers.

So this game has a set of guidelines too. You may go, "Well, that's not how I learned it in psychoanalysis." Or, "We didn't do that in yoga class," or TM, or AA, or whatever. Okay, you're right. But, like Lou Reed said, "Hey, babe, take a walk on the wild side." Let's do it.

Game Guidelines — The Short Form

1. Healing is an inside job. We've got all the power we need to move us toward wholeness, right inside ourselves. The main tool our inner healing power uses is our awareness, or consciousness itself.

2. To play Movie Yoga, we'll use our APS (See Chart on page 41: Awareness Positioning System™). To picture your APS, imagine a plus sign: The horizontal arm is everything outside of us. The vertical arm is everything inside us. The reactions we have to a movie come from the outside, from the horizontal. But all our healing comes from the inside, from the vertical. So, we don't blame the film, which is outside us. We take all our movie reactions, and look inside to see what got triggered. Once we accept it's an inside job, we're free.

3. Almost all movies contain at least one of four universal stages of transformation, what we call the *Death/Rebirth Matrix* (see chart on page 80). So be looking for these stages when you play. Every time you feel one of these stages, it's like you're visiting a unique world. Here are the four stages: the *Safe Zone*, the *Trapped Zone*, the *War Zone*, and the *Free Zone*.

Moving Toward Wholeness
Where We Get Guideline Number One

Let's start at the meta-level — the big picture. We're all always moving toward wholeness. This is not some great new realization I came up with. A lot of philosophers and seekers have been saying this for thousands of years. We can have all kinds of experiences in which we feel more whole than we may have before. And then later, after doing more life, we'll have some other experiences where we feel a sense of even greater wholeness than that. For example, when you were seventeen, didn't you feel like you knew everything? And then when you were twenty-five — if you are that old — didn't you feel like, "Oh, my god, I was so dumb when I was seventeen"? And so on.

What seriously speeds up moving toward wholeness is when we make a conscious effort to make it happen. Like therapy, yoga, meditation, dance, prayer, or whatever we do to make ourselves feel better and be happier people. It's like moving over into a faster lane of traffic when we do any of these things. And some practices really get us flying — sort of like meditating on a freight train, a teacher once said. Just think of moving toward wholeness as doing something for ourselves that's healing, or freeing, or empowering.

The Inside Job

Moving toward wholeness is also an inside job. We have the key to transformation totally within ourselves. Everybody. There's a power within us — doesn't matter what we call it — might be the soul, the higher self, whatever — that has our complete best interests at heart. It's working all the time.

But for simplicity's sake, let's just call this power the Inner Healer. It's responsible for letting us know what needs to be worked on or healed in order to reach our highest and best self. And the way the Inner Healer does this for us is by bringing issues, memories, universal truths, and all kinds of insights and experiences into our awareness at the right time.

Awareness itself is a healing power; by awareness, we mean consciousness. We have to become aware of something before we can transform it or get a real benefit from it. This isn't really very radical, either. Just about any therapist will tell you we can't heal from something until we know what the thing is. We all have patterns inside us that we have either never been aware of, or have forgotten. And all these issues build up inside and end up motivating us in ways we have no idea about. We think we're all free people, making clear choices, and acting independently. Except that's not exactly accurate.

We're all caught and limited by unconscious issues inside ourselves. What we really have is a kind of longer or shorter leash. So the more of our self-imposed limitations we can release, the longer the leash gets — the more freedom we have. Until, maybe one day we're off the leash. And then, when we make a decision, it really is based on an authentic experience of freedom that we actually do have, instead of just thinking we do.

For example, some of us are just natural loners. We enjoy being by ourselves better than hanging around lots of people. We're not distressed by other folks. We just prefer our own private company. Then there are those of us who are alone because we're not comfortable with people. We get panicky in a crowd, self-conscious around others, hate going to parties, and dread weddings and airports. We would rather get a poke in the eye with a sharp stick than engage in a little social repartee.

By the same token, some of us are just born 'people persons'. We're cool with being alone, too, but it's just not our first choice. Then there are others of us for whom being alone is actually quite a challenge. Or worse, being by ourselves makes us so anxious, we just can't stand it. We basically hide out in crowds. We seem to need other people in order to feel safe, or to give us a sense of identity.

If we are one of those who are challenged either by being alone or by being with people, there may be unconscious underlying issues that are influencing how we feel. But whether there are or not, we are all apt to create our life styles in ways that deal with, or compensate for, our fears of being either alone or with people. We may convince ourselves that we love being single when in fact we are terrified of relationship. Or conversely, we sing the praises of our love for companionship when in fact we'd be with anybody just to avoid having to wake up in the morning alone.

What I'm getting at here is that we think we are free people making free choices. But, in fact, we are on that leash I've been talking about. In this case, the leash is our fear either of being alone or of being with people. In either situation, we convince ourselves it's just our choice, our preference, to do what we do. But our choice or preference is not free. It is limited by our fears. Our sense of freedom is at least partially an illusion. But the good news is that by making our fears conscious, or by becoming aware of them, we can gradually lengthen that leash we've been on, or get off the leash altogether. And then, eventually, we can become truly free.

The Buddha Problem

If healing is an inside job, what's the purpose of the outside world? After all, it's pretty much where we do all our living, right? I mean other people, all our relationships with, well, everything — people, places, things — they're all outside us. So how is this consistent with the idea that healing is an inside job?

As long as we focus on something or someone outside ourselves — or believe that our happiness or well-being depends on any of these things at all — we can never be truly fulfilled. If we do this — rely on something outside ourselves to change in order for us to feel better — we'll always be slaves. We'll always be giving our power away to the world.

If focusing on something outside ourselves is how we believe we'll get free — and believe it or not, most of us have been taught this since we were kids — then we're basically screwed. It's a no-win situation. Why? Because all seven billion people on the planet are doing the same thing. Everybody believes you get happy by making other people, places, and things do what you want.

So, we're bound to run into serious trouble when what we want gets in the way of what somebody else is going after. The best we can hope for, then, is some temporary happiness, which we had to fight for in the first place. And which, on top of that, we have to fight for again to keep from losing. I get depressed just thinking about it.

The person who explained this problem the best was probably the Buddha. He said suffering is caused by craving, by unfulfilled desire. Either we don't get something we want — and that makes us unhappy — or we get it — and then we're worried about losing it. And either way we're unhappy all over again — right away, or in a few seconds, hours, or days, when we start desiring the next thing. But again, the problem is that we're dealing with this whole external playing field, where everybody on planet Earth has got an angle. And why not, if that's how we believe we can get happy.

By the way, a tried-and-true screenwriting axiom sums up just about every flick like this: *somebody wants something really bad and is having trouble getting it*. Think about it — action adventures, romance, horror, comedies — whatever — including life. It's scary how right-on that is. We've all got what I like to call the Buddha Problem.

The Awareness Positioning System™
Where We Get Guideline Number Two

Okay, so if we start with the game plan we've been laying out so far — happiness comes from within, etc. — what would have to be different? The way we deal with outside reality would have to change. We'd need to have a radical new outlook in relation to people, places, and things. And the source of this revolutionary outlook turns out to be one of the most vital functions of the Inner Healer. This previously undiscovered resource is the power in us that facilitates this fundamental reorientation of ourselves. It's what I call the *Awareness Positioning System*™, or *APS*.

Ever been lost on the road? Driving wherever, maybe even back where you started, absolutely clueless — totally turned around? Then you pulled over and studied that maze-like map from your glove compartment, or your downloaded computer print-out? Not much faster, was it, than what we might imagine the old astrolabe days must have been like, when seafarers spent a large part of their time checking out the stars. That is, if and when they could see them.

The Game

Or, better yet, have you ever had a chance to activate your new Global Positioning System, your trusty GPS? Then waited a minute or two while magic happened, while you got tapped into some off-world satellite that oriented you to your spot on planet Earth? Then, *voila*! In the voice of your choice, some invisible cyberspace avatar lays out before you in insanely accurate detail exactly how to get where you're going, and asks you what you want to eat or what movie you want to watch before you get there.

Think of your APS like that, only it's not about some outside journey down an interstate. The APS is a different type of magic entirely. It's like going down an 'Innerstate': one that can orient us on those inner journeys we're taking all the time. Those odysseys of feelings and longings, frustrations and satisfactions, that seem to be the key to whether we are fulfilled or not and are at the core of who we really are.

All this getting lost on the thousand-and-one inner roads to nowhere, and trying to find our way out of one mess after another, is a pretty accurate metaphor for how we attempt to find happiness. The problem is, most of us, for most of our lives, have been using old, clunky, out-dated strategies for getting the fulfillment we feel we deserve. So, just as the GPS has almost miraculously simplified road travel, the APS can do the same for us on our many adventures down what the Alcoholics Anonymous tradition calls the "Broad Highway." I'm talking about all the paths — and I mean every one — we take in life itself.

Here's how our APS works. Imagine two intersecting, rotating vectors in three-dimensional space, like on a radar screen which — okay, stop right there. Here's where you say, "You've got to be kidding! Vectors in blah, blah, blah! I got enough troubles negotiating my life already. Any new system worth my time better simplify the mess I'm in, not make it more complicated." And you know what? You'd be right as rain.

So, let's rewind. 'Chapter Two' of our APS definition: Imagine for a moment that human beings are innately wired to be fulfilled, even if the overwhelming evidence of our past experience so far tells us that we are, in fact, total screw-ups. And how about I leave out the three dimensional part and make it just two dimensions, like on a piece of paper. Okay, now imagine that this innate wiring that I call our Awareness Positioning System™ operates like a plus sign. That better? And guess what? You even have a diagram. If you need some help visualizing this, turn to page 41. The horizontal arm of the plus sign — the one that goes sideways — represents how we relate to the outside world — the world of people, places, and things. As we said, this is where we mostly focus. It's where we look for our happiness. In fact, until we have a consciousness-shifting experience, for many of us it's the only arm there is.

But check it out: If this is all that we are, then if we use this plus sign metaphor to understand our Awareness Positioning System™, we don't have a plus sign at all. We have only a minus sign. Now this says something important about living life based only on the horizontal arm. It seems to say that there's a minus, meaning that there's something missing. That we need another dimension in order to be whole.

In order to make a minus into a plus, we need a vertical arm, too. The vertical arm of the plus sign — the one that goes up and down — represents us and our own nature. From the point where the arms of the cross intersect downwards represents my internal being — my feelings, my patterns, the way I've become accustomed to thinking and operating in the world. It represents what I'm aware of about myself and also what I'm unconscious of. It symbolizes my personal psyche.

Okay, the upper vertical arm of the plus sign upwards — above the place where the arms intersect — is also me, but something else. It represents my reaching and longing for some idea or feeling that I may have about my higher nature. We could call it our spiritual aspirations, our concept of a higher self, god, or goddess or whatever. Anything we reach toward when we feel moved to do that sort of thing. So this vertical, up-and-down arm is what we look to for our healing when we're doing transformational practices.

Most of us go through our whole lives giving little or no attention to the vertical dimension of who we are. We focus on the horizontal — what we want from other people and situations. We do this until we're forced to look inside, either by something negative and stressful, like deep emotional or physical pain, addiction, some serious angst, or by something powerful and positive, like a spontaneous experience of the sacred — something like that. But usually, we have to be absolutely desperate before we stop seeking our happiness 'out there'.

Seeking exclusively 'out there' can give us only temporary satisfaction amid trouble and pain. If we first seek our happiness through inner means — on the vertical arm of our nature — then it's possible to feel happy in any number of outer situations. Because then we know that external things are temporary, whereas inner realizations can always be relied on.

The implications of our very own APS might seem at first glance kind of radical. But just because we've never used our Awareness Positioning System™,

The Awareness Positioning System™ (APS)
How the Outer World Can Lead to Inner Transformation

↑

Relationship with Self and Wholeness
Sources of Inspiration
The Inner Healer
How we make our memories conscious
and heal them

← **Relationship with the World**　**Relationship with the World** →
People, Places, and Things　　　People, Places, and Things
Emotional and Psychological Triggers | Emotional and Psychological Triggers

Relationship with Self
Our Unconscious
Our Memories
How we are triggered

↓

or even known there was such a thing, doesn't mean we've never had one. In fact we've all had one forever. You know how GPS is optional on a lot of cars? Well, APS comes standard on all human models. All we have to do is activate it, bring it on line. Give it a test drive or two, like we would any kind of technology. We just have to orient ourselves to its amazing possibilities. And then we will never, ever have to be lost for too long, no matter how confusing or circuitous the life adventure we may be on seems to be at the time.

Don't Blame Me

Let's look at some additional features of our newly discovered APS. There's another serious downside to living only on the horizontal arm of the plus sign. By mistakenly believing that happiness is an outside job, we then feel that pain is an outside job too. By that I mean, when we feel bad, we blame somebody else, or an outside circumstance.

Remember the expression, "The devil made me do it?" This was an exaggerated way of saying what we actually do say all the time. We really do believe that our feelings change because of what someone else does, or something that happens to us. For example, we say, "You made me angry," or, "If it wasn't for you doing such and such, I could be happy." And a thousand others like that.

What if, instead of seeing all our emotions as being caused by something out there, we saw every 'horizontal' experience — with whatever person, place, or thing we come in contact with — as an opportunity to grow, to learn something about ourselves? What if we saw all these interactions, not as *causes* of our condition, but as *triggers* — signals or signposts that could then lead us to discover the real causes of our reactions? Which, guess what, are inside us, on the vertical arm of who we are.

Okay, so far: The real causes are inside us, on the vertical arm of who we are. This changes completely how we see the horizontal — the world playing-field out there. Now "outside us" becomes an infinite field of opportunities and triggers for us to grow. Hmm, going to need a little more?

All right, here's an example: Let's say, as a child, every time I went for the second piece of candy or cake, my Momma told me I was being greedy or selfish. So maybe in therapy I get in touch with some anger, possibly some shame, and some sense of low self-esteem. Perhaps I have a pattern of denying myself pleasure, or maybe I'm even sabotaging myself in my current relationships when it comes to getting what I think I need.

Through the Eyes of a Child

The First One — or at least the first I remember — was Twenty Thousand Leagues Under the Sea. *It was Saturday morning. I might have been four. I don't think we even had our first TV yet — or maybe just. I think it was just my sister and I — no parents. I remember we came in in the middle of the movie. In those days, it wasn't that big a deal to me. Not like now, when if I miss one nanosecond, it's time to abort the film. Only two things I remember about that movie. One was a scene, and the other was a feeling.*

What I can still see was that Eye — the eye of the giant squid. And the hero — I think I learned many years later it was Kirk Douglas — fighting the squid from the deck of some ship — might have been a submarine. And waves were pounding the deck. I can actually remember my mouth being open. Because what I was feeling was Awe.

I was, like, swept off the deck of my own ship – my own reality — by waves as fierce as the ones knocking Kirk Douglas around. I was transported. And, you know what? I think, for the first time in my short life, I felt home. Swept into the land of archetype, of myth. And to this day that world has been more real to me than anything I've felt in this world here. That's just the way it is for me. No wonder I love movies. They're my bridge to home.

Now, in my current life, I'm at a party, and we're all having fun. And I reach for the last brownie, and my girlfriend says, half-joking, just cutting up really, "Oh you little pig, oink, oink." And then she kisses me and laughs, but I'm not laughing with her. I'm dying. I'm all shamed out; big huge waves of anger are washing over me. I hate this woman. I think, "She hurt me. She abused me. I'm going to leave her. I can't trust her. I'm always getting hurt by women. I think I'm going to be a monk and give up sex and chocolate." Okay. Now that's me a tad overreacting. You think?

So what's the deal here? Let's use our new guidelines — especially the Awareness Positioning System™ (APS) — to check it out. Basically, I have two ways I can react to this situation. One, I can blame my girlfriend for hurting me, and then I can retreat, regroup, or run. Probably just like I did the last five times something like this happened. By the way, this is a damn near foolproof way to stay single for a long, long time.

Or I can bring my APS online, like this: "Whoa, that hurts. Okay — light bulb. Here's a big-time trigger that I'm experiencing on the horizontal arm of the plus sign — out there. How do I know? Because my reaction is way out of proportion to the actual situation. I've got to be letting some serious underlying issues mess with my head here to want to throw away my relationship based on this."

So where do the issues come from? They come from within my own psyche. If I want to bring them fully into my awareness, I can look down the vertical arm of the plus sign, into my own life, into my past, where I already have insights into this sort of thing happening previously. Now, this can be harder than it sounds, because it is way easier to blame somebody out there than it is to go sleuthing around in my own psyche, even if it's not about blaming myself. But let's say I do it, even if it's tough. And because I've dealt with this issue before, I can take it pretty quickly to the deepest place I know so far — like following a string of beads.

The string is the pattern of half-familiar emotions, this thing I know so well — in this case hurt, shame, and anger. Two ways I can deal: one's me blaming life — the horizontal arm of the plus sign — out there. The second one is owning responsibility — the vertical arm of the plus sign. Big difference.

It doesn't mean I have to blame myself. We're not saying that people don't do hurtful things to us. In fact, I wish the word *blame* just did not exist. It's not about blaming anybody — somebody else, or ourselves. That'll never free us. It's about doing the practical thing to transform ourselves, so that we can feel better in the world. As I was saying, we let go of the blaming mode — ourselves or others — and we trace the feelings down the vertical arm of the plus sign. And when I do that, I end up with that situation where I reacted to how my mother treated me when I was little.

Through the Lens, Brightly

There's something else to it too. Check out this scenario: Let's say that I have a history of feeling abandoned. Now that's a difficult pattern. It's like a lens we look through that colors our outside experience. And abandonment is a tough lens to have to see the world through. Okay, I'm at this party — the same party — and I've just shamed myself into not eating that last brownie. And my girlfriend gets up and goes to the kitchen.

Now, her getting up and going to the kitchen is an essentially neutral act. She's just doing her thing. It doesn't have anything to do with me. Unless of course she's really the Wicked Witch of the Milky Way, she knows I have this pattern of abandonment, and she's out to totally screw with my head — but let's assume that that's just a totally paranoid reaction, and she's really not like that.

But what do I do? I have a melt-down, and feel — what? Abandoned. She just abandoned me. Why do I feel that way? Because I'm looking through the lens of abandonment, that's why — not because of anything she actually did. See what I mean? Can you imagine how complex this co-creation of our realities can get? And that's just two patterns — this one and the one about the brownies. We've all got way more than two. Mix all those up and that lens becomes an intricate kaleidoscope.

We think we're free, but as long as we're just reacting to situations from our lenses, we're not. What we're going to do in our new game is take this life practice of using our Awareness Positioning System™ and apply it to how we look at and experience movies. How many times have you said, "That movie or that scene freaked me out; pissed me off; scared the hell out of me; made me cry; disgusted me; offended me," or whatever? As if all this was in the movie. Did you ever consider that maybe a million people saw the same movie as you? But you might be one of the few who reacted the way you did?

Okay, what does that tell us? That the power of our emotions is not just in the movie itself. It's inside us. Whatever lens we ourselves are looking through at the time will at least co-create what kind of reaction we'll have when we see the film projected on the screen. We have to realize this fact if we're going to do Movie Yoga.

One more time, so as not to miss it, this is Movie Yoga: We sit on our sofa, like Aristotle would have if he had had a sofa and a TV, watching the old tragedies. We activate our APS. And through our awareness — our consciousness — we observe our reactions to the movie — not just to the whole film, but to all the parts. Every reaction we have. And instead of then blaming the film, we look at ourselves. We go inside.

We find what it is within us that has been triggered by the scene in the movie. We travel in our consciousness down the vertical arm of the plus sign to its source. Get to the experience — the original event or cause, at least as deep as we are able. Then, in whatever way feels right, we bring it back up the vertical arm to our heart. We embrace it. We may reach upward at this point, on the vertical arm of the plus sign, and call down some inspiration we know. Or, if we don't have a source we know of, maybe we open to the Great Mystery. Whatever works or feels right. Then we let it go. And that's Movie Yoga.

THE ZONE
CHAPTER 5

Private Witt: *I seen another world. Sometimes I think it was just my imagination.*

~ The Thin Red Line

Gimli: *Certainty of death. Small chance of success. What are we waiting for?*

~ The Lord of the Rings: Return of the King

Ofelia: *My name is Ofelia. Who are you?*
Pan: *Me? I've had so many names. Old names that only the wind and the trees can pronounce. I am the mountain, the forest, and the earth. I am...am a faun. Your most humble servant, Your Highness.*

~ Pan's Labyrinth

Okay, you're on board so far. But what about this thing called the Death/Rebirth Matrix? So, it's about time to get a feel for the four zones in our Movie Yoga universe — these stages or seasons of transformation just about every movie contains in one way or another: the Safe Zone, the Trapped Zone, the War Zone, and the Free Zone. When we are experiencing one of these spaces, it can literally feel that we are in a fully-realized world, with its own rules and unique operating systems.

Learning how to use our understanding of these four stages of life to transform ourselves is one of the great contributions of my dear friend and mentor Stan Grof. For many years we have shared, among other things, an intense passion for movies. And I owe much of my understanding of moving toward wholeness to the many adventures we've gone through together.

First, let's try to get a deeper feel of what it's like to think in terms of these zones. It may first help to imagine we're space wayfarers mapping new planets. So when we get to some rock, we're checking it out. What's the atmosphere like? Any greens? How about the critters? Is this place carbon-based? Silicon? Mercury? If you mapped it, when you go there later just to chill, you won't be blind-sided. What you're expecting should be consistent with what you already found. You could handle it, no problem.

You are not going to expect this new planet to be like Earth, where we get three-dimensional space and time, and a strange, cantankerous bi-ped doing its best to destroy everything. Different place — different parameters. Same way with the Four Zones in the Death/Rebirth Matrix. You figure out the parameters — then get what you expect. The longer you play, the more you can rely on them, the more they'll become your allies. The more you'll start seeing how just about all your life experiences fit into one of these zones.

Film Appreciation 101 — Oh Boy

While we're laying the groundwork for the zones, we should first mention just a couple more things about Movie Yoga in general. Truth be told, a lot of us wouldn't know a feeling if it hit us upside the head. All too often, our minds keep us blowing smoke — hanging out on some fantasy cloud. Or living, as one famous author said, just a few inches from our bodies. Sure, the intellect is important, and we need those powers that come from there, in order to be fully integrated. But in Movie Yoga, what's going to give us the full ride are our feelings.

Movie Yoga's not some film class at college either, a gray matter head trip where we mentally deconstruct a movie, do some kind of intellectual analysis of what the director's trying to say, or what are the camera angles or the lighting. It's not even 'cinema therapy', where, if you have an addictions problem, let's say, your therapist would recommend you see *28 Days, Clean and Sober,* or *Leaving Las Vegas*. That's good therapy, but kind of linear. Movies — any kind of movie for any kind of problem — can be so much more. So, for this game, forget all that. Remember, the worst movie ever made can be the one that changes your life.

Looking through the lens of the four zones can be like somebody just parted a veil, letting us get all kinds of revelations we never knew were there. I remember a night I spent a long time ago with a musician named Berry Oakley, who was the bass player for the great rock band, the Allman Brothers. He was like a mentor to me.

This was just after the Allman Brothers' first record came out, and we shared an apartment building together. We sat up all that night, listening to some of the greatest rock music of that time. And while we listened, Berry pointed out the things that he loved, that made it special for him as a player, especially the bass line, what holds it all together. And that night I felt I heard and experienced music, in a sense, for the first time.

That night, music became even more of a revelation than it already was, if that's possible. This is exactly what we want to have happen here with movies. Sometimes it just takes getting something pointed out to us — as though we all of a sudden see something out of the corner of our eyes, and another universe opens up we didn't know was there. The reason we can suddenly see it is because now we know what to look for.

I hope, if you do Movie Yoga, you'll be able to experience movies with new sensibilities, new eyes and ears. When the lights go down, it'll be like we're becoming better and better pitched tuning forks, instruments the movie can play. To play out our poetic metaphor a little more, the whole purpose of this game is to quicken us, to enable us to sing our own personal song of transformation. And this new satisfying way to live life will be jump-started by those special resonances that movies can help us feel.

Death/Rebirth Matrix moments resonate because they're based on the unique experiences of our own life journey, which the film we are *feeling*, not just watching, re-enacts in us, for our eyes only, like a private screening. So, as we paint the picture of these four stages, keep in mind that it is how they *feel* that characterizes them. They'll show us something we already know deeply: about how we've been in the transformation process, dwelling in these four zones, our whole lives, through all kinds of challenges and triumphs, even if we didn't know it at the time.

Sitting on a Whale

Sometimes when we get to what feels like the core of a pattern of deep emotions, we learn something amazing about our psyches — our inside worlds. Instead of just being about this life — from when we are born up to the present — the psyche turns out to be way bigger. We can have experiences that aren't just about our current life.

For example, one of the universes we can visit is that place that Joseph Campbell wrote about, the universe of mythology, the land of the great epic stories that are common to us all. In fact, Campbell said one time that Freud, who taught that our personal life was all there was, was "fishing while sitting on a whale"; that's how big the psyche really is.

> *Another name for this same big universe that kind of overshadows our small personal, separate worlds is the* collective unconscious *that Carl Jung described and named.*

So, here we go: try to imagine times in your life when you felt the feelings and sensations I'll describe.

First, safety: it might be like everything's cool — no worries, just kind of drifting. The idea of starting a project, setting out on a physical or mental journey, is not yet even in the picture. This is before the urge to change, where we get that itch, even begins to stir us up; we're just hanging out like a fetus in a good womb. No place we need to go. Nothing we need to do. Not until we hear, as Joseph Campbell would say in talking about his "Hero's Journey," the "Call to Adventure."

Second, next thing we know, we're all stirred up, antsy. The walls begin to close in, and suddenly we're trapped. Some force in us, or outside us, wants us to grow or change, but we're not ready. We're being pushed and pulled at the same time. This force can't be bargained with. It absolutely requires us to leave the safety of the womb, or home base. But the mental or physical power to get cranked up — to make this thing, this journey, happen, is just not available to us yet. Trapped, alone, misunderstood — not yet out of the womb, but not yet in the birth canal, not yet on the road, not yet taking charge. Wishing we could hole up, but knowing we have to function. Any of this ringing a bell?

Okay, third: struggle, or war. We take the leap, get kicked, start moving, pushed by that thing, whatever it is, inside us or outside us, some relentless creative force that has a plan we can't fully perceive. We're out of the womb, definitely in the birth canal. The depressed, no-way-out mood we felt before has shifted, and now we're motivated by power, something too big to stop, maybe even aggression. We're heading for the light, a goal we can maybe finally glimpse, but it's a battle. The outcome is up for grabs. We have to get courageous, overcome all the forces that hold us back, fight against what doesn't want us to succeed. We might not make it. It can feel like the world's against us. We, or our whole plan, may die, go up in flames. Through the battle, right up to the gates of victory, we may even feel like we've failed, like some kind of death, where we just can't finish, can't go through with it. That's struggle. That's the war.

And fourth: when we least expect it, or even when we are expecting the worst: we're free. Like, how did that happen? We've made it, just when we thought all was lost. We come through. We get born. The struggle's over, and we're free at last. We are home, after a hard-won victory. We may even feel that we've left some old part of ourselves behind, as though it has died. And in some strange way, it has, and a new self has been born to take its place.

There it is, in four quick paragraphs, what a few psychologists and many mystics have written a million words about: one timeless, universal process that all of us human beings go through over and over. Some systems call it death and rebirth. I know I do. If we think back on our lives — really focus, get as honest as we can — to any major crisis we've ever gone through, victory we've won, or didn't, or challenge we've faced, we'll see one or more, or all of these four zones in the adventure we went through during that challenge.

Remember, it's all about the feelings. All of us have spent time in these zones. That's why it's so important now, so relevant. And now that we've taken a peek behind the curtain, just like when Berry Oakley schooled me in the nuances of rock and roll, it's going to be one serious eye-opener how often movies are filled with enactments of these four zones. But the real eye-opener is when we discover we're the ones up there on the screen, laughing, crying, dying, and being reborn.

Mystery Schools

Another wonderful thing about death/rebirth experiences: they show us that life is cyclical. Cultures have constructed societies based on death and rebirth for thousands of years. Most of the great religions refer to it in one way or another. In many early cultures, including Greece and Egypt, there were hidden practices called mystery schools, where participants would attend in secret. There they would do rituals designed specifically to take them through some kind of experience of death and rebirth.

So, for each of us, there are some of these grand, over-arching cycles of death and rebirth that mark incredibly important endings and beginnings. These are the ones that might be more challenging to go through, because the stakes seem so huge to us, the outcome is so important. Then there are all kinds of lesser or mini-cycles that we go through each day like the "Convenience Store Odyssey I related earlier.

Know what a movie's creation begins with? An inspiration in the heart or mind. Know what the process of physically creating that movie begins with? A blank page. Guess who had the inspiration? Who sat in front of the blank page? You got it. A human. Movies reflect at least some aspect of the human predicament, the universal struggles and triumphs and tragedies that we all go through — just like Aristotle said about plays.

If we play this Movie Yoga game a while, we're going to really understand the universal story arc that a screenwriting teacher nailed too: "Somebody wants something really bad and is having trouble getting it." Absolutely. There's the time when you're in a not-wanting zone — that's peace: the Safe Zone. But you know that want and longing are going to come. And you see no way to get that thing you desire. You're stuck. This is not the safe zone. This is the blues. This is the Trapped Zone.

But after what feels like eternity on that barren rock, there's that light way down at the end of the tunnel. You glimpse a way through, but you're going to have to fight for it, in the War Zone. Then just when you think you'll never make it (you may even have to surrender, give up ever getting it, and go through the death of your dreams and aspirations) you come through. It's a new dawn. It's a new day. A new world: the Free Zone. Rebirth.

The Death/Rebirth Matrix

So we know that there are at least two dimensions to the psyche: the personal and the collective. But guess what? That's not all. There's one more. And this is the one that we're really interested in right now. It's the dimension where, if we explore deeply enough, we can find all our experiences of death and rebirth. But not only that, it's also the place where we have the memory, or record, of our biological birth. And this death/birth dimension acts very much like a doorway between the personal and collective. So we call it the Death/Rebirth Matrix — that part of the Movie Galaxy that has the solar system with the Safe Zone, the Trapped Zone, the War Zone, and the Free Zone.

Transformation is about moving toward wholeness — moving from a limited experience of who we are and then expanding into a larger perspective of what it means to be human. So, the death/rebirth experience we've been talking about is how moving toward wholeness happens. It's the way we move from just *thinking* we're only separate individuals on planet Earth, to *having the experience* that our individual self is just one part of who each of us is. To put it another way, death/rebirth is how we each make the big leap from being just a separate individual in a world of other separate individuals to being united with all beings and all life. And this sense of union, or oneness, comes from the collective dimension, which includes everything that we call the Great Mystery. And, when it's all said and done, this Great Mystery is what many movie yogis report they want to get yoked to.

CHAPTER 6

I LAUGHED, I CRIED

Jack Lipnick: *Can you tell a story? Can you make us laugh? Can you make us cry? Can you make us want to break out in joyous song? Is that more than one thing?*

~ *Barton Fink*

Li Mu Bai: *I would rather be a ghost drifting by your side as a condemned soul than to enter heaven without you.*

~ *Crouching Tiger, Hidden Dragon*

Cartman: *That movie has warped my fragile little mind.*

~ *South Park: Bigger Better and Uncut*

When trying to account for all the possibilities of taste, most people agree that there's at least a gender difference in movie preference, otherwise we'd have never heard the term 'chick flick'. For example, Cary will see any romantic comedy, even the ones that look from the previews like they're going to be pretty awful, and even if you can tell the entire plot just from the title. She doesn't care.

I, on the other hand, will go to any halfway decent, or even $1/100^{th}$ way decent, vampire movie. Okay, I'll go to *all* vampire movies. Except PG-13 ones. I'm sorry. Vampires are just hard-wired to be "R"-rated. Anything less, and there go the fangs and all that red stuff. Vampire flicks are just built-in "epic". Any time you're dealing with being dead, but undead, and living forever with all kinds of powers, like flying, having super strength, and serious animal magnetism, plus you get to bite pretty women in the neck, or men, depending on your tast, that can't be all bad.

So what's this got to do with Movie Yoga? I hope it's getting pretty obvious: What we like and dislike about certain movies usually has something to do with our insides — the feelings that get triggered when we see films. So, just because we don't like a movie might not be the best reason not to go see it. It could be that our tastes are actually telling us something about a certain film's healing possibilities for us. The one we have a special dislike for might actually rate pretty high on the 'heal-o-meter', if there were such a thing.

By now, you know what I mean when I say, "feelings that get triggered, or come up." I'm talking about all the feelings we could have watching a movie, like:

I hated it

I loved it

I laughed

I cried

I got so pissed off

I got excited

I was overwhelmed

I was mortified

I felt shamed

I got embarrassed

I was disgusted

Or how about:

I was terrified

I felt high

I got turned on

I felt dread

I felt relief

I experienced unbelievable joy

I felt one with all humanity

If you've ever enjoyed movies in your life, you've no doubt felt some of these things. And that's what keeps you coming back.

Confessions of a Fan

Ever waited hours in line for a movie or concert? Why do we do this? Because we're fans, that's why. Because we have passion. You know that excitement you feel just before the lights go down? And then right after? We Movie Yogis live for that moment.

Obviously, I'm someone who seriously loves movies. And it's not surprising that so do my wife, Cary, my sons, my closest friends, and many other friends, colleagues, and people I've gotten to know through my workshops and trainings. But, as you can probably imagine, I clearly like some types of movies better than others. Of course, I can appreciate any really well done movie.

Now, appreciate *doesn't mean I* love *them. But, no matter what the genre, I can love them, as long as they're great. And here, by "great," I mean they have to be intense. They have to have* that *magic. That magic is my personal indefinable set of criteria — just like the one you probably have too, which would be different from mine, but just as valid and sacrosanct. And I can love a movie, even if it's tough for me to watch. And I can admire plenty of films, or at least something about them, even if I didn't particularly enjoy seeing them.*

Bryn and I have a rating system we've used since he was really little. It goes like this: At the bottom comes, "We hate it." Next up on the scale, "We like it." After that, "We love it." Then, "We loveitloveit," and then, "We loveitloveitloveit." Highest praise is, "We adore it."

For years, the first time I would see a movie in the theater, I had a way to tell how I felt about it before I was even aware of it. It was the M&M's barometer. I always had M&M's at the movies. I could enjoy a movie and keep right on eating them. But for a really great movie, the M&M's were going to get put down. And if magic happened, like this film was becoming one of the hundred movies in my 'top ten', the theater was filled with a sound like someone's necklace just broke, and the beads are bouncing and rolling downhill through the aisles. That was me, leaning forward spilling the M&M's.

But besides my particular reaction to individual films, there are genres I feel the most attracted to: action adventure, horror, sci-fi, film noir, mystery, and basically anything truly epic. And there are some that are always last on my list — usually romantic comedies and dramas about dysfunctional families. The same is true for virtually every moviegoer I know. I mean, not that they have this same list of favorite genres, but that they have their own special list.

I Laughed, I Cried

Cary, Bryn, and I have a tradition of getting together with two close friends, who are brothers, on Oscar night. Sometimes one of us has to work and can't make it. One year I was even in Hollywood pitching some screenplays. I was in a hotel right on Wilshire, basically at kind of ground zero. Now that was weird. But whoever can make it each brings their Oscar picks and their top ten and bottom ten movies for the year, and we each take turns reading them aloud.

Each of us sees up to a hundred or more movies in the theater each year, and many more at home. And the ever-fascinating thing is that, while there is some overlap, there is always a pretty wide variety between all our different lists, in both the top and bottom ten. There are always movies that appear in the top ten list of one person and the bottom ten of someone else. So it's really interesting to see, even among a small group of friends, how different our movie likes and dislikes can be.

Among professional critics, there's definitely a wide range of reactions to the same film. You can get a good picture of this from going to the website rottentomatoes.com and looking up any film. It lists numerous reviews for each movie, and indicates whether the reviewer found the movie "fresh" or "rotten." There is even a one-to-a hundred scale giving an average of all the reviews, called the "tomatometer".

We're going to "see" a lot of movies pretty soon in this book, so consider this next section a kind of practice, or warm-up. Ready?

Okay, let's say I'm a novice Movie Yogi. It's my maiden voyage playing this game. Now, remember, you may see a lot of movies that you don't feel much about one way or the other. But what's the point? By its very nature Movie Yoga only works if you end up caring about at least something in the film. Or, for that matter, caring about the fact that you didn't care a bit. So, let's start with one kind that we have feelings for, the one that blindsides us. No, wait a tic. We'll come back to this. We have a problem.

Spoiler Alert

One of my unwritten rules of Movie Etiquette is that nobody, and that means *nobody*, can say anything, and that means *anything*, about a movie I'm going to go see. Never at any point; not one word. I hate having anything in my consciousness about a film. Call me a little eccentric. This may come as a surprise to you, but it's worse than eccentric. You might say obsessed.

I have this overwhelming problem with movie trailers: I'm addicted to them, yet I won't watch them. Somebody needs to shoot the people who make the trailers these days. Hell, three quarters of the time, once you've seen the trailer, you don't even need to see the movie. I've actually seen parts of scenes from the final minute of a thriller in the trailer. It's criminal. I'm serious.

The problem for me is that whatever image I've seen, or line of dialogue I've heard, becomes indelibly imprinted on my psyche. So when I'm watching the movie, it's impossible for me to not be thinking about and looking for what I saw in the trailer. It totally ruins that brilliant mystery, the discovery moment of seeing the film burst upon me from out of nowhere. That moment is magic, and I don't want it contaminated by wisps of pre-coded memory that cloud its spontaneity.

Now, the other side of this problem, and one reason I'm addicted to trailers even though I refuse to see them (unless I'm positive it's going to be a film that's totally inconsequential to my life), is that some trailers are pure art in and of themselves. They exist as masterpieces independent of the films they're designed to sell. When that's the case, I just adore seeing them, just like I'm seeing a movie. I can be transported in a short time, no matter what I may end up feeling about the actual movie. Sometimes the trailer's great, and then so is the movie. But I've seen some trailers that blew my mind, and the movie sucked.

You see the dilemma. So, if you were sitting behind me in the theater, and the trailers were coming on, here's what you'd see. This otherwise normal-looking man suddenly throws down his popcorn, covers his ears with his hands, lowers his head, begins to rub his ears vigorously, and starts to utter something incoherent. The rubbing of the ears helps mask the sound of a good THX system. The mumblings are actually some Hindu mantra that keeps my mind from trying to hear the dialogue. I know it looks a little funny. But hey, this is a deep practice. And it's tough being a Movie Yogi on the lunatic fringe.

Now, though, I'm going to have to violate all my rules. For the rest of the book, I'm going to be talking about segments of films — very important, integral pieces — that'll ruin the movie for you if you've seen the pieces as a result of trying to play Movie Yoga, like I'm definitely going to recommend — that is, if you're a maniac like me. So, here's your official spoiler alert.

One recommendation I have would be to rent any flick I mention and see it in its entirety before you proceed with the yoga. But my guess is, since you all are more than likely movie freaks too, like me, that you've probably seen most of them anyway. But please consider yourself warned. And I deeply apologize to you and the movie gods and goddesses if I offend you or them in any way so that it might screw up my already pretty precarious movie-watching karma. So, here we go. Here are a few examples that cover some of the more likely scenarios you'll run into when you head to the cineplex to play Movie Yoga.

In Which I Go to See a Movie I Think I'll Probably Like, but Don't Think I'll Get Blown Away By

Let's say I'm your average guy out on a Saturday night. I've seen a preview for something that looks pretty good. The reviews are decent — a couple of stars, a thumb up or two, and over 50 on the tomatometer at rottentomatoes.com. A couple of reviewers I usually agree with like it. And it's one of my genres, say an action movie. So I sit down with my popcorn, my M&M's, and my drink and watch the movie. It's going well enough that I get a pretty good pulse. I'm on board from the "git-go". There's a cool hero, or anti-hero. There's at least one hot girlfriend. The bad guys are pretty damn bad and worth getting worked up about.

I'm feeling all this stuff, right? And, as the movie rolls, things get out of hand, or, at least for me they do. One of those things that just destroys me — I mean activates the hell out of me — looks like it's going to happen. The hot girl whom I like a lot gets into some serious jeopardy. Okay, now if this is one of your everyday Hollywood things, it's more than likely she's going to live. I mean, almost die, but make it. So, I probably don't have to sweat it too much, do I?

Now, so far, as a Movie Yogi, I'm doing pretty well, rocking along, doing and feeling pretty much the same thing I always would in a movie. But here's where the wheels come off. The girl I really care about DIES! I'm going, NO WAY! I can't believe that just happened. All of a sudden, I'm seriously out of the comfort zone. My world's rocked. I'm freaking out. My insides are all mobilized. Feelings are jumping all over themselves to get into my awareness — sadness, disbelief, devastation, loss, fear of the end of my comfort zone, and distrust in the nature of the cosmic order. Okay. Now what just happened?

Light bulb. I got triggered. No, you think? Especially since my movie buddy sitting next to me is just kind of shaking his head — like, what's the big deal. Obviously, the death of a beautiful woman you care about is not one of his major issues. But, it's sure as hell mine. Now, what's that all about? This is where we play Movie Yoga. My alarm just went off — Opportunity to heal! Opportunity to heal! Time to bring my Awareness Positioning System™ online. So, now I get to check it out. Maybe not that second. Maybe I stagger out of the theater first. Or maybe I tell my buddy what's happening. But what am I doing while I'm talking to him? I'm opening myself up, and letting the feelings flow through.

Now, it's possible I've done some work in therapy on this issue. Except, for me, there's no situation in my life. I check it out with my APS™ down the vertical arm of the plus sign, and there's nothing there in this lifetime. I didn't lose a girlfriend, a sister — nothing like that. But, wait a minute. It's definitely happened in movies before. Like David Fincher's *Seven*, where in the end the evil guy, played by Kevin Spacey, cuts off the head of the sweet woman, who is Gwyneth Paltrow, and gives it to her husband, the Brad Pitt character. Now that totally screwed me up.

And so did one of the fifty or so horror flicks I saw — a nasty little thing from Australia called *Wolf Creek* where horrible things happen to both the women characters, whom I seriously cared about. So, this is no isolated bummer. Where else could this be coming from?

Oh, yeah, what about the collective? Come to think of it, I get this feeling that my reaction might be archetypal. But I still don't really know. Maybe I get a sense that it has something to do with the way I feel about being separated from the archetypal Mother. Only then do I start remembering things about being separated from my actual mother in this life. Or I begin to have feelings about the nature of the Divine Feminine itself, and what that may mean to me. Maybe I even get a hint about my birth, feeling separate from my mother in the birth canal. Or that my being born might kill her. Who knows?

So, I'm getting a few clues from my Inner Healer that I'm on the right track. The one thing I know for sure is that the death of the woman in the film brought up something seriously meaningful for me that obviously has some important implications about my life. Even if I'm not certain what all these implications are, even if it's still a mystery to me, I already feel better. Because I'm not caught in this no-win trap about blaming the flick. I'm not a victim of the movie. I can do something about it. I can withdraw my energy from the outside situation and take it within myself. And that fact alone feels good.

It feels good to be taking charge of my life, to be empowering myself, to not be blaming others. And to feel that I'm on an adventure of healing, not just stuck in some kind of painful loop that I'm doomed to keep feeling for the rest of my life. I begin to realize that the journey is about me, and that I hold the keys to my own transformation. I know that it's probably going to happen again. I mean, beautiful women that I care about are not going to stop dying in movies just because it upsets me.

But the next time it happens my Awareness Positioning System™ (APS) might just come on automatically. I'll go, "aha" (light bulb) — here's my pattern again. And this time I'll feel perhaps a little different, with a little more insight. So, what have I done? I've just played Movie Yoga. And I thought it was going to be your average, no big deal Saturday night.

In Which I Go See a Movie I'm Looking Forward to, but Know I'll Be Freaked Out by

Here's another situation, the next level of Movie Yoga. You know how I feel about vampire movies. But besides that, I love all great horror movies, even though there's a serious double-bind built into the experience for me. Here's the problem: If they're bad, then I don't get scared to death. And that's a good thing, right? Well sort of. Because, then, that means they didn't work.

I guess I'm actually kind of relieved when I'm not freaked out, but disappointed too. Because getting freaked out is the point. If the movie is good, I get the hell scared out of me. And as a Movie Yogi, what happens when I get the hell scared out of me? I get to be conscious of my fear via my APS. I get to dive into it, fully experience it, see what it's bringing me, and where it comes from in my psyche. And how it connects me to other people who go through the same things.

This was what happened to me in 1978 when the first *Alien* movie came out. It was directed by the master, Ridley Scott. There was this incredible buzz about the film — about how terrifying it was going to be. And how we were going to see things we'd never seen before on film. And there was a lot of secrecy about what went on when they were filming — about how even some of the cast were kept in the dark about a couple of things. What a set-up. When I went, I felt a little bit like I was going to my execution. I was scared to death, but kind of thrilled too — that thing that happens with good horror.

Now, I went with some friends. And this was one of those magic experiences where we were all on the same page. Not only that, everybody in the theater was too. This wasn't *Jaws* — where there was also this communal thing — plenty of a sort of up-tempo excitement. And it wasn't *Star Wars* either, or *Lord of the Rings* — again, that pop cultural phenomenon kind of thing happening where you knew you were a part of something huge.

No, this was different — communal, but not the same. Everybody was sort of quiet. There was definitely a kind of excitement in the air, but it wasn't manic (like the first day of *300,* the Alamo-type Thermopylae tale, and *Dark Knight,* when the San Francisco Imax was jam packed with rabid fans, or Watchmen). It was more like an undercurrent of collective dread. A sense that we were all on the same ship, and that we knew it was going down, except not exactly when. We were like a bunch of doomed travelers. We all knew we were in for something bad. We were sure it was going to be a special kind of terror. And, you bet, it felt kind of cool.

We were all there for exactly that reason. We all wanted to be there. And yet we all didn't. See what I mean? I'd felt that way before in a horror movie, but never had I been with an entire group of people who were sharing that same thing. I'm saying there was a pall of fear, doom, and excitement hanging in the air like incense smoke. Quiet. Too quiet. Edgy. Shared death waiting to happen.

It did, too. That special moment did come. The John Hurt character had just got freed up from the disgusting octopus-looking alien thing that had been clamped over his face, sucking up his life through a tube down into his stomach. So, he and the crew are all relieved, and they're eating dinner. And all of a sudden, the Hurt guy starts to choke. So they lay him out on the dinner table. And then that thing happens: His chest explodes, and the baby alien pokes his head up, looks around, and hisses — that baby alien hiss that'll soon turn into the grown-up alien hiss that would be a trademark for alien films to come.

Rumor has it that only some of the actors knew this was going to happen. So the look on their faces — of total surprise, disgust, and fear — doesn't look a lot like acting. I've seen the film maybe fifty times, and it still doesn't look like acting. Anyway, the little alien critter just scoots off, leaving all of us in the theater and everybody else up on the screen just staring dumfounded, in shock, not believing what we'd just witnessed.

Now, if you're young, and you've seen a lot of horror movies, but you've never seen *Alien,* or maybe you just saw it, because it got re-released, you say, like, "What's the big deal? That kind of thing happens all the time in horror movies: you know, monsters hop out of stomachs." And you'd be right. It does happen all the time. But this was the blueprint; this was where it all began, at least in an "A" film sort of way. And I'm telling you, it was terrifying. And activating.

Okay, so how was it activating? Well, if all of us in the theater were doing Movie Yoga when we saw this scene, and our Awareness Positioning Systems™ were online, there's no doubt some pretty intense emotions would come up like those I've already mentioned. But how many of us would have been able to say that this brought up a personal memory from inside them? Like, "Oh yeah, that's because I remember the time the alien popped out of my chest and sprayed blood all over me and my friends at the club." See what I mean? So where does this kind of terror come from? What activates us so bad about this? What triggers us?

Here is another situation where we'd have to look into the collective to find some kind of meaning and validation for our powerful reaction. And you know what it was for me? You might be able to figure it out, given the focus of much of this book. If you were thinking it might have something to do with death and rebirth, you'd be right. It's about birth — some kind of horrific, twisted, dark mutation of birth. A birth from the dark side, where it's not just some cute little cuddly baby human that comes out, and there are angels in the room, and everybody weeps with joy.

We're talking about another kind of birth altogether: the birth of evil into the world. Like *Rosemary's Baby*, or Damien from *The Omen*. And that's just plain terrifying. It strikes fear into the heart of us all at that place where we are connected with the archetypal nature of the Dark Side. This is why it grabs us. What's scary is that it shakes up our safe world, where birth, at least after we get through it, and it goes well, means something sweet. All of a sudden we are confronted with the possibility of the opposite of something sweet. We basically get our cages rattled pretty well.

It'll force us to face every nightmare we ever had, every situation where we felt something go bump in the night, or in the middle of the day for that matter. That kind of experience can act as a summons from our psyches. It is a call for every challenging memory we have ever had, every time we've ever been scared, or had something bad happen to us, to come up into our awareness. And this is why it can be incredibly healing.

Because we've all had something scary or painful happen to us. And we've learned even from traditional therapy that, in order to be healed from these things, we have to bring them up, make them conscious. So, here it is again — Movie Yoga. We purposely choose to watch a movie, even though we know it may scare us or activate us. But if we are courageous, we can have more than just a fright. We can have a healing. And that's what Movie Yoga is all about: having powerful experiences in a movie that at the same time can be healing.

Where I Go to a Movie I Swore I Wouldn't See in a Million Years, Even Though I Know It's "Good", but It's Going to Bring Up a Bunch of Stuff I Spend Most of My Life Trying Not to Think About

You might ask why would I even go near a movie like this. Well, lots of reasons. Maybe it's supposed to be a masterpiece, has some major buzz, or even an Oscar nomination. It's more than likely going to be seriously intense, which pretty much trumps all other criteria. Like I said, intense is part of that magic. Maybe Cary's dying to see it, and I've already used up my last three turns to pick the flick. Also, I always just love doing things with her, so that's a good enough reason right there. And maybe — he said, thinking fast — if I see a Cary flick (like, sacrifice myself for the good of the relationship) it's just possible I can get her to reciprocate, even though I'm still in movie debt — like, convince her to go with me soon to watch something go Boom!

Or it could just be because I'm a Movie Yogi, and feeling suicidal enough to be willing to see minutely what feelings and reactions it brings up in me. Let my Awareness Positioning System™ and my Inner Healer shine the light of conscious awareness on them so I can continue my journey of transformation. And there's always a chance I'll love the movie. Really, it could happen.

Anyway, for me, this is the type of movie that's the real 'horror' flick. The kind where you're in someone's house, with their family, and their family is really messed up. Intense dramas about family dynamics. I'm not kidding; I go crazy in there. I really can't deal with them. Why? Well for one thing, because of my childhood, which was the World Cup of family dynamics. And when I'm in one of those, squirming in my seat, thoroughly preferring to get a poke in the eye with a sharp stick, I often find myself doing How-Not-to-Dive-Into-a-Movie Yoga.

I can tell you every crack in some theaters' ceilings, every stain in the stage curtain. I've studied them all, while my special hell breaks loose on the silver screen. I make a serious effort to get my attention off the screen and focus anywhere but up there. Ah, the pleasant distraction of people munching on popcorn, the screaming of babies, clueless idiots talking on cell phones. I'm hoping to tune into some distracting conversation, some avid texting, which I would usually consider heinous violations of the movie-going code and subject to contract hits, evil spells, and much worse.

So I have to consciously remember that I'm a Movie Yogi, and drag my attention back to the film, at least a fraction. I experience the excruciating pain of the hapless protagonist and his unbelievably bad home life, or of the horrible tension between family members, the sarcasm, the torture, or whatever. I identify with, say, Igby, the lost soul in *Igby Goes Down*, the kid who, with his brother, plans the mercy killing of his sarcastic, controlling, vicious mother. The kid with no moorings, no sense of home or safety, who wanders through the streets of New York looking for any kind of haven or home base he can find which would make up for the thing he never had.

Or I relate to either of the two brothers who get shuttled back and forth between their parents in *The Squid and the Whale*. The dad — angry, controlling, sarcastic, bitter, and selfish. The mom — oh so liberal, touchy-feely, yet ultimately self-absorbed. Or Lars, from *Lars and the Real Girl*, who, because of the trauma of the loss of his parents, feels unbearable pain just to be touched and who is so afraid of relationship that he creates one with a sex doll.

Or I just avoid what's happening. I close my eyes and think about unicorns — any damn thing — even a date with the Inquisition — which would be mega better than paying attention to the monster nuns in *The Magdalene Sisters* as they torture the young women who've been sent there by vicious, abusing men. What was it the Ellen DeGeneres fish character said in *Finding Nemo*? "Just keep swimming, just keep swimming." For me, in the theater with this flick, it's like, "Just keep breathing, just keep breathing." Or sometimes it just gets down to, "Breathe in, breathe out. Repeat."

Then, in those few brief flashes of courage that may come over me, I activate my APS, focus it as sharply as I can, and allow my feelings to emerge. And then, oh lord, here I go, down the vertical arm of the plus sign into a world I know so well — my own family. The great dark thing I try to avoid at the movies. The thing, however, that I've been willing to look at for many years, through traditional therapy and alternative healing methods. So, why the hell not?

And when it really gets bad, I'll bring up, along with the painful memories, an image from the first family dynamics movie I can remember: *Ordinary People*. The archetypal dinner table — for so many of us, the scene of the crime. The boy, Timothy Hutton, and his parents, Donald Sutherland and Mary Tyler Moore. Just your every-evening family get-together, no big deal.

The camera moves around the table, face to face, back and forth. The "what did you do today?" banter, the excruciatingly painful attempts at light-heartedness, at the "everything's-okay-ness". And, you know what? It's looking pretty okay. Until the camera pulls down below table level. And we see the kid as he white-knuckles his chair, desperately holding on for dear life. While up top, in family land, everything's hunky dory — just another evening around the table with blinders on as evil spells float back and forth.

One more interesting thing, though: that image has stayed with me, not because it causes me so much pain by reminding me of what it was like for me growing up. It's imprinted on my psyche because it's such a powerful validation that I am not crazy. That I am not alone. That what I went through is something that other people have been through and have survived. Instead of separating me from humanity, it connects me. I'm in good company.

Now, this is cheap therapy. Buy the flick, rent it. Watch it. Or any of the hundreds that do that thing for you — whatever the thing is for you that turns you upside down, that has the power to change you. This is Movie Yoga at its toughest, but at its best. Thank you, Robert Redford, for *Ordinary People*. Thank all of you in the Hollywoods everywhere for putting your souls on the line for us all in these brave and painful films.

Tears

Crying used to be excruciatingly complicated. First off, I was a sensitive little fellow. But that wasn't too safe in my family. My dad was one of those "Be a man" kind of men, which says a lot about what he went through growing up too. I only remember one or maybe two hugs we ever had — plenty of firm handshakes though. They had to be firm, because this was what guys did.

But what went on in the movie theater, in the dark between me and the screen — well, that was my turf. And Bambi *was where it all started — my first movie tears, in what has become a deep and lasting lifetime tradition of movie tears. When his momma got shot — whoa. Was that close to my little boy's home, or what? I mean, lose the mother? I'll never forget Bambi standing all alone in the snow. Sure, the great protector stag emerges from the gloom to stand by him. But, I'm sorry; it's not the same as the mother.*

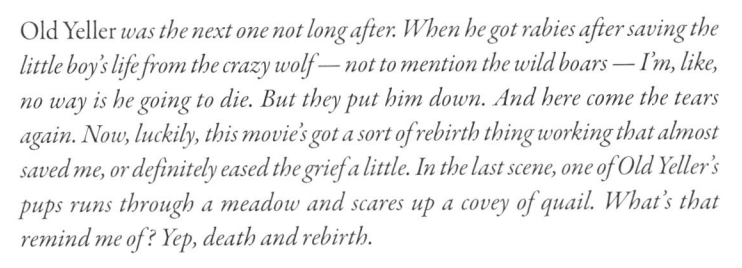

Old Yeller *was the next one not long after. When he got rabies after saving the little boy's life from the crazy wolf — not to mention the wild boars — I'm, like, no way is he going to die. But they put him down. And here come the tears again. Now, luckily, this movie's got a sort of rebirth thing working that almost saved me, or definitely eased the grief a little. In the last scene, one of Old Yeller's pups runs through a meadow and scares up a covey of quail. What's that remind me of? Yep, death and rebirth.*

But it was tough around my house, and I learned to shut those tears down. Made a yoga out of it, actually. So, I quit crying, except with a little chemical help now and then, like drugs and alcohol. I mean, I could get plenty sad. In fact, I was sad most of the time. And the tears would come up, but they wouldn't come out. They'd get right out into my eyes; they'd get wet. But that's as far as they would go. It's what they call frozen tears in some kinds of therapy. So it wasn't until after doing a good bit of work on myself that I could cry, except for one time.

You guessed it. It was in a movie, One Flew over the Cuckoo's Nest. *It was at the end, after they'd lobotomized the Jack Nicholson character. And he's lying up in the bed, all drooling, his soul already gone. And his Native American friend (played by the great actor Will Sampson) smothers him with a pillow, because it was a tragedy that such a bright light almost could be put out, but then hang around so dimly lit.*

And after that, he took a water fountain, and threw it through the window and escaped. I just couldn't handle it. The tears washed up out of me. And I have to tell you, for them to come so strong from that dammed up, dead place deep inside me, it had to have been a colossal outside trigger. And One Flew over the Cuckoo's Nest *was it. It was about busting loose. It was about freedom.*

Oh yeah, I forgot. I cried twice more during those frozen-tears years. The times were real close together. I was nineteen. I believe I was just beginning to wake up spiritually. The first was Elvira Madigan, *a Terrence Malick-type Swedish film. A lovers' tragedy. And the second was* Bonnie and Clyde, *another lovers' tragedy. At least that was the lens I was looking through. These two movies were a wake-up call. I never looked at film the same way again after that.*

There have been other milestones since, when movie watching went to a whole new level. Peter Weir's Gallipoli *did it. And* Bladerunner *changed me forever. So did* The Matrix. *I better stop now, because this is about tears. But this that-movie-changed-everything list could go on forever. Come to think of it, after the frozen tears thawing out years, the crying list and great movies just go hand in hand.*

Just wondering: How many of you cried during Terminator? *After Sarah Connor and Kyle Reese, the warrior from the future, made love, their hands clasped in a James Cameron kind of way, with the unstoppable terminator out there somewhere tracking them down. Reese said, "I came through time for you, Sarah. I love you. I always have." Just remembering that now, I can hardly handle it. Epic, pure epic, all the way.*

Where I Try to Convince Those of You Who Can't Stand Violence That Violent Movies Can Be Transformational Too

Now here's a crossroads. Many of my fellow Movie Yogis report being totally on board up to this point. But this is where the wheels just about come off. Why would we want to go to one of those incredibly violent films when we have such strong values about how harmful they may be? How about because we're Movie Yogis through and through? And because the philosophical underpinnings of this game are totally valid, even for this challenging issue. So far, we've been through the warm-up flicks, the somewhat difficult-to-watch films, and even some personally very painful ones. We've at least imagined, and maybe even begun to seek, the positive benefits of bringing up difficult emotions into the light of consciousness. So, let's take what we've looked at so far, and see if any of it applies to this loaded issue.

The explanation I'm going to give here is based on something I see all the time, especially at workshops. But I've also witnessed it in many circles where people are intelligent, thoughtful, and usually spiritual individuals. It's one of the main challenges I have introducing people to Movie Yoga. It's the intelligent, sensitive, spiritually-minded person who has sworn to avoid violence in the movies. So why is that?

The main reason is that no sane persons want violence in their own lives. And the bottom line is, people feel that if they see a violent movie, they'll somehow be participating in creating more violence in the world. How good people arrive at this conclusion makes a lot of sense. First of all, we've all experienced some kind of violence in our lives, either a little, or possibly a great deal. It has happened physically, emotionally, or mentally. It has been perpetrated by someone close to us, by strangers, or by some more impersonal aspect of society in general. Not to mention, birth is basically violent too, and we've all been born, anatomically, if not emotionally. Yes, violence has been done to us. Or, let's be honest, we ourselves have actually done some violent things, or participated in the occurrence of violence in some way, for which we more than likely feel some measure of shame or guilt.

So, obviously, seeing violence in movies — both the victim and the perpetrator aspects of it — actually does exactly what you would expect from our study of Movie Yoga: that is, it brings these kinds of emotions and experiences up for us. And the way we deal with these patterns and feelings, even though they may be extra-intense and loaded with all kinds of negative implications for us, is exactly the same as when we deal with any other pattern from our unconscious.

Since this is the case, it begins to be clear how this would be an extremely valuable use of Movie Yoga. If we get activated by the violence in movies, it's just like anything else. We are being afforded an excellent opportunity to heal those situations where we've had violence in our lives, either what was done to us or what we've done to other people. And since none of us are immune to the effects of violence, one way or the other, it makes radically good sense to have another effective tool in our tool kit to help us deal with it.

Now, what about the question of indirectly creating more violence in the world if we go to violent movies? A number of reputable studies have found no causal connection between acts of violence and watching violent films. But the research notwithstanding, are we assenting to or participating in the continued spread of violence in the world, if we go to these movies? Most therapists will tell us that we tend to act out those things that we haven't looked at that are hidden inside ourselves, in our unconscious. Carl Jung called those patterns within us, which we haven't looked at, the *Shadow*. And when we're acting out these things we are unconscious of in ourselves, he calls it disowning the Shadow.

So, instead of being afraid that if we see violence in the movies, we'll be participating in or adding to violence in the world, the exact opposite is actually true. If we can use our Movie Yoga strategy with our reactions to the violence that we see in the films — how we get triggered when we see it — then we can heal those places inside ourselves where we have experienced violence at some point. And then, like Jung and the vast majority of therapists are saying, we won't be disowning our shadow.

We won't be acting out those things we haven't looked at. We won't be participating in creating more violence in the world. Because, if we play Movie Yoga at the theater, working with our reactions to violence, we're actually looking at what part we ourselves have already played in how violence affects us and others. Then we are making these patterns conscious. And the payoff is, once these things reach the light of consciousness, they lose their power over us. Then we are way less likely to act unconsciously, thereby harming others with either physical or emotional violence. And we'll also respond in everyday life situations with less fear and more freedom. We'll be freer from those unconscious knee-jerk aggressive reactions we used to fall into. Less apt to get caught in those current situations which we used to perceive as threatening because of violence that was directed toward us in the past.

Where We Visit the Village of the Happy Nice People

But let's look at violence in films in another way. One of movies' non-negotiables is that they're all about conflict. And another lens to take a look through is that violence is just the most extreme form of conflict. Even comedies are full of violence. Not only is there the obvious slapstick, but most forms of comedy contain some type of psychological, physical, or other type of violence, often all mixed together. Take the most romantic comedy you've ever seen. What good people do to hurt each other — dishonesty, withholding love, causing emotional pain— is consciously or unconsciously violent, even if they don't bash each other over the head with a board. So we just can't avoid conflict — not at the movies, not in real life.

In case we just blew right on by this mega-important point, I'm going to repeat myself: *Movies are about conflict. Conflict.* I'm sorry, but too much conflict is just not a valid criticism in this game. I remember one well-known critic dissing *The Lord of the Rings: The Fellowship of the Ring*. Know what he said? He said it had too many adventures. Cry me a river! That's like going to see a comedy and not liking it because you laughed too hard. I mean, I'm pretty forgiving and open-minded about all our idiosyncrasies, when it comes to having feelings about films. But having a problem with conflict is one challenge we're just going to have to work through.

In screenwriting school they teach writers to "put your heroes up a tree and throw rocks at them. And then keep throwing bigger and bigger rocks." Remember the statement we used about both movies and life: somebody wants something really bad and is having trouble getting it. Would you really care about a film if your heroes were just always mellow and unruffled and didn't want much of anything, one way or the other? How lame is that?

Like they say in film school, would anybody go see a movie called *The Village of the Happy Nice People*? I remember reading somewhere that if it weren't for adultery — some hot and heavy, clandestine, forbidden sex — there wouldn't have been any such thing as the nineteenth century novel. This may sound kind of harsh, but if we have problems at movies because we feel too much, well, that's just a great place to start our own personal Movie Yoga.

Where We Get a Preview of Movie Yoga for Couples

Some wise person once said that anybody can go sit on a mountain top all by themselves, meditate for twenty years, and get all spiritual. It's tough, but doable. That same person also said that one of the toughest paths of all is relationship yoga. This one's not for the faint of heart. So, how would this yoga work? You would use exactly the same principles we've been talking about for Movie Yoga.

Every time you react to what your partner says or does, the practice is: you bring your APS online, you don't focus on him or her, but withdraw your energy from the horizontal arm of the plus sign and take it inside — down the vertical arm. Try not blaming your partner for everything in the universe, and you'll understand exactly what this wise guy meant by relationship being so tough.

But what about Movie Yoga? Is there any way it can actually keep us couples from going at it whenever some conflict emerges around differences of opinion concerning movies? You bet. Well, except I'm not talking about those minor squabbles over turning the living room into an Imax theater. Or spending the next three months' rent on the down payment for your twelve-channel surround sound. Or getting the platinum, super-deluxe-for-special-people cable package with three hundred and eighteen channels, when you know for a fact that your partner only watches ten channels, even though he or she says you never know when the other three hundred and eight might come in handy. Hey, this isn't a panacea. You're all on your own with that stuff.

But I would like to share with you one situation where Movie Yoga was an amazing eye-opener for Cary and me. And really helped us understand each other a lot better. I read an interview one time where a movie star called his movie star wife a team player because she got him some very special movies that he liked for Christmas. Well, Cary's a team player too. By that, I mean she's not at all averse to going to many otherwise guy flicks, as long as there's a good chance that the movie has some redeeming features, other than that they go Boom!

For example, she's seen and really liked some of my favorites, such as *Terminator, The Crow, Dark City, The Thin Red Line, The Matrix* (all three), *Kill Bill* (both), and *Pulp Fiction* — but not *Sin City* or *300* — not no how, not no way. But it works both ways. I've sat through, and really loved, a whole lot of Cary flicks, like *Pride and Prejudice, Love Actually*, just about anything with Colin Firth, Hugh Grant, or John Cusack, *Room with a View, Romy and Michelle's High School Reunion, Fifty First Dates*, and all Merchant/Ivory films.

But here's a time when things didn't go as planned. For me, any new Ridley Scott movie is an occasion for celebration on a galactic scale. And since Cary knows this, and because she loves me, and likes most of the Ridley Scott flicks I'd dragged her to in the past, she agreed to see *Gladiator* with me on opening day. Remember my family's movie rating system? Well, on that day we covered the continuum. I was on one end. I adored it — that's top of the line. And she was on the other — she hated it. It doesn't get any worse than that.

Now, silly me, I thought that the reason she didn't like it was because of the intense violence. And since I thought that was the case, I was prepared to argue with her, because there have been many times where a movie had just as much intense violence as *Gladiator*, or more so, and she actually loved it because there were so many more redeeming features.

But that's not why she hated it. I mean, there was a lot that she said she could have loved — after all, it was Ridley Scott — if it wasn't for one major thing. A story point. It had to do with the way they wrote the main character Maximus, played by Russell Crowe and for which he won an Oscar.

Here's what pisses her off to this day: After Commodus, played by Joaquin Phoenix, kills his father, the emperor, played by Richard Harris, so he can be the new emperor, he asks Maximus to join him and lead his legions. Maximus knows that Comadus is a worthless scumbag, so he refuses. And because of his refusal, Comadus then has Maximus' innocent family murdered. This basically destroys Maximus' life and sets up the action for the rest of the film. He's a broken man, who, Cary saw, let his stubborn pride and shortsighted sense of honor cause the death of the family he loved. A classic response from your typical man afflicted with testosterone poisoning.

What he could have done, Cary believed, was go along with Comadus, let Comadus think he's on his side, just for a while, thereby saving his family and still being able to thwart Comadus and save Rome in the bargain. According to Cary, he let this almost laughable pride, as well as a kind of male arrogance, get in the way, all of which ended up being the cause of his tragedies.

Now, that just flabbergasted me, because I was going through something totally different. One of the thousand reasons I adored the flick was directly and specifically because Maximus did what he did. Here's how I saw it: I saw Maximus as being totally filled with honor and a sense of duty — to his family, whom he adored. But also to the Emperor Marcus Aurelius, and to Rome.

So, I saw him as a great tragic hero in the Aristotelian sense. What caused his downfall — and the death of those he loved the most — was the conflict created by his extreme sense of loyalty and honor. He couldn't lie. He couldn't be false. And this honor was what destroyed his family and himself.

What made it so amazing to me was that I could identify with Maximus, with the dilemma of an honorable man trying to be a straight shooter in an otherwise bent society. And it was this very sense of his striving for honor, and making an honest mistake by perhaps being too rigid, that caused his downfall. But I really went through a catharsis with him. And I continue to do so, every time I see the movie.

Now for a while, I tried to convince Cary that she saw it wrong. This was the source of quite a few lively discussions we had. And let me tell you, there's nothing more pathetic than me when I try to tell Cary she's wrong. Because, guess what? She wasn't wrong. But neither was I. We were both looking through different lenses. And in this case, the lenses we were looking through happened to be two rather opposite archetypal reflections on the nature of the masculine in the world — one from a masculine perspective, and one from a feminine perspective.

On the one hand, Cary saw Maximus' rigidity as a classic example of a particularly male reaction, which ends up causing great pain and suffering to the innocent ones around him. And I saw his honor and his conflict as being an archetypal example of what men must face in the world today — the double-bind between family and work — and attempting to do the right thing, to be honorable, but then getting screwed for the attempt.

Now the issue here is not which one of us is right. We could both just as well be out in left field. But this serves so well to underscore the power of unique and separate perspectives that are both sacrosanct in their own right. Can you see how rich Movie Yoga can be? I mean, I've learned so much from Cary over the years, and this was just another piece of it. Our differences of opinion here and in so many other cases have enabled me to break free of my own rigid boxes (just like the box she says Maximus was in) and see the world from another perspective. I usually go kicking and screaming, but in the end I can get there most of the time.

So, I just wanted to point out here an extra added benefit of doing Movie Yoga. And this is to enhance Relationship Yoga. Not only am I getting triggered by my reactions to the movie. In this case I got triggered by my partner's reactions! So now my Awareness Positioning System™ is smoking! I have my hands full on the vertical arm of the plus sign — as long as I can get past that age-long tendency I have to want to say it's always Cary's fault. But really, I know she's not to blame. I'm pretty in touch with what's really going on. Actually, as I alluded to in an earlier chapter when we were talking about blaming the outside world for our problems, would you buy, at this point, that it was the devil who made me do it? Didn't think so.

PART II

LIGHTS, CAMERA, ACTION

CHAPTER 7: GETTING SEATED

Elwood: *We're on a mission from God.*
~ *The Blues Brothers*

Jasper: *Everything is a mythical cosmic battle between faith and chance.*
~ *Children of Men*

Frodo: *I know what I must do. It's just that I'm afraid to do it.*
Galadriel: *Even the smallest person can change the course of the future.*
~ *The Lord of the Rings: The Fellowship of the Ring*

Okay, let's watch some movies. Oh yeah, we got to slow up one more time. There's a problem. You're reading this book. And we're at the part where we take an in-depth journey through the four zones of the Death/Rebirth Matrix, itself, including Death, and point out some amazing pieces of films that reflect parts of this process. So now, you ask, "Are we going to just talk about movies?" And I say, "You bet. It's a book, isn't it? How else are we going to do it?"

And then you say, "That's just lame. All this about getting down with movies, really experiencing them, and now we're just going to talk?" And then I say, "No kidding. You're right. But I'm not a magician." And then you say to your runnin' buddy, "Come on, girl. Let's go see a real movie." And you know what? You'd be right. I wouldn't blame you for putting down the book.

So, given that we have this dilemma, I hope one of three things will happen. Either you'll check the list of movies we're going to discuss, and then take a break from the book, go out and rent or buy one, and then watch it. Or else, you'll read the chapter and hopefully get excited. And then, go out and rent or buy some, and watch them either for the first time, or again, with new eyes this time. Or, third, check the list, get the DVDs or Blu-rays, and watch just the parts we're talking about, one by one, all the way through the death/rebirth journey.

Remember, you are looking for sections labeled "Test Screenings" to watch movies. Boxes of text contain interesting highlights, if you want to go deeper. To make the process of watching and reading simpler, the next section is a cheat sheet, a "Cliff's Notes" of Movie Yoga. That's so, if you really want to play, you won't have to go thumbing through everything you've read up to now looking for the good parts. You'll also notice the accompanying chart on the Death/Rebirth Matrix. It should help make things easier, too.

The Short Form — Redux

1. Healing is an inside job. We've got all the power right inside ourselves that we need to move us toward wholeness. The main tool our inner healing power uses is our awareness, or consciousness itself.

2. To play Movie Yoga, we'll use our Awareness Positioning System™ (APS), a kind of GPS for awareness. Imagine a plus sign: The horizontal arm is everything outside us. The vertical arm is everything inside us. The reactions we have to a movie come from the outside, from the horizontal. But all our healing comes from the inside, from the vertical. So, we don't blame the film, which is outside us. We take all our movie reactions, and look inside to see what got triggered. Once we accept this, we're free.

3. Almost all movies contain at least one of four universal stages of transformation, which we call the Death/Rebirth Matrix. So be looking for these stages when you play. Every time you feel one of these stages, it's like you're visiting a unique world. Here they are: the *Safe Zone*, the *Trapped Zone*, the *War Zone*, and the *Free Zone*.

> **Biological Birth**
>
> *There's getting to be more and more research out there about babies being able to remember things that happen in the womb, and how the birth process actually plays an important role in the way we develop. It'll be great if one day, scientists will proclaim, "Humans can remember birth."*

Getting Seated

But until they issue a statement like that, many of us already know we can have experiences within ourselves that feel as though we are reliving our birth. We already know how important birth is to our lives. On top of that, we are also aware of the fact that these experiences can be incredibly healing.

When researchers like my friend and mentor, Stanislav Grof, author of Psychology of the Future, *were mapping the death/rebirth process, they discovered something awesome. It turns out that these four aspects of transformation in the Death/Rebirth Matrix paralleled four stages of the actual physical birth process. In other words, physical birth and transformational birth seemed to follow the same pattern.*

So, when we are talking about death/rebirth, we can also at the same time be talking about physical birth. And when we have an experience of death and rebirth, whether it's at a movie or doing some other kind of practice, it's likely that these two levels can be interchangeable. So healing can then be happening at either one or both levels at the same time. Also, the feelings and imagery we get seem to be interchangeable. And if you think about the dynamics of physical birth or death/rebirth in general, there seems to be a special kind of logic where this mutual interchangeability makes sense. You'll see this really clearly in just a little bit.

So, let's do it. Let's take a journey through some movies. As the Tom Hanks character said to his platoon in *Saving Private Ryan*, on D-Day, fifty yards off Omaha, just before the door went down on the landing craft and 50mm machine gun fire tore half of them to shreds, "I'll see you on the beach."

THE SAFE ZONE

CHAPTER 8

Pocahontas: *Mother, where do you live? In the sky? In the clouds? The sea? Show me your face. Give me a sign. We rise, we rise.*

~ The New World

Comadus, watching Lucius sleep: *He sleeps so well because he is loved.*

~ Gladiator

Chance: *As long as the roots are not severed, all is well, and all will be well in the garden.*

~ Being There

Richard: *And me, I still believe in paradise. But now I know it's not some place you can look for, 'cause it's not some place you go. It's how you feel for a moment when you are a part of something, and if you find that moment...it lasts forever.*

~ The Beach

Peter Pan: *When the first baby laughed for the first time, the laugh broke into a thousand pieces, and they all went skipping about. And that was the beginning of fairies.*

~ Finding Neverland

As we go through the zones, let's thicken the plot. This ought to make our experience of them, and the associations we make about our own lives, that much richer. So, what we'll do, instead of just describing the zones as the psycho-spiritual death/rebirth process, we're also going to add the parallel process of physical birth. Check out the chart on page 80 for more information if you need it.

Like we said, the Free Zone is heaven. It's about feeling safe — maybe like being connected to the mother, either our physical mother, or perhaps even the Divine Mother. It's about getting our needs met — food, love, and so on. It corresponds to when the baby's in the womb. So, when something triggers us and these kinds of feelings come up, we might experience it metaphorically, like a heaven. Or we could experience it biologically, like hanging out as the fetus in this warm watery universe, the unborn baby connected to the mother. Or we simply feel content, safe, and cared for.

I mentioned Joseph Campbell's "Hero's Journey" earlier. But in case you skipped that part, it's the life adventure he says we all go through every day, in whatever we're doing, that is actually a roadmap for transformation. George Lucas first brought this to the general public's attention in *Star Wars*. He reported that this was the framework he'd used in making that movie. It's probably one of the main reasons why the film had such a global appeal. Just about everybody loved it. Well, there's also a close connection between the Hero's Journey and the death/rebirth process that we're using.

For example, the beginning of the Hero's Journey is like being at home, where we then get the "Call to Adventure." It's very much like the journey of death and rebirth. In the birth process, home — or at least the first home, the one during the pregnancy — is the womb. And when the birth process begins — whether it's biological birth or the transformational journey that'll take us through death and rebirth, we also get a call — the call to be born.

The problem is just that, in order to be born, we have to go through an intense struggle. So, in the womb, or at the beginning, we are at a level of innocence — sort of pre-adventure. This is the "I don't need to worry because all my needs are being met" place, or a sensed, "Why should I struggle?" Ever felt that? Some of you will say yes. Oh, you're saying no? Actually, this is the zone that many people can't relate to, because all they can remember when they look back is pain. There are a couple of reasons why this is so.

First, what we're saying is that it's not always a good womb before we set out, whether it's a journey for physical birth or transformational death/rebirth. There's another possibility: what we call a "toxic womb." We might hate where we are, because it doesn't feel safe like it's supposed to. We don't feel connected. It may feel dangerous where we came from; some of us experience it as the womb, others as our family after we're born. So, in this case, taking the Hero's

The Death/Rebirth Matrix

	The Safe Zone	The Trapped Zone	The War Zone	The Free Zone
Archetypes and Images	Oceanic ecstasy Heaven Paradise Connection Oneness Unity with the Divine Mother Innocence	Cosmic engulfment Hell Timeless suffering Meaninglessness Dark night of the soul Existential crisis Separation Aloneness Guilt/Inferiority Insane asylums Concentration camps	Volcanic/Dionysian ecstasy Purgatory Light at end of tunnel Meaningful struggle Death/Rebirth Power/Aggression Sexuality Demonic experience Wild adventurer Warrior Apocalypse/Armageddon Harems/Carnivals	Cosmic ecstasy Coming home/Oneness Sudden, unexpected breakthrough Rebirth Spiritual homecoming Divine Child with Mother Glorious nature End of war/Revolution Oneness/Safety Radiant light, colors Love/Humanitarianism Liberation
Biological	GOOD WOMB Symbiosis Oceanic/Watery Connection with mother through umbilicus Emotional and physical needs met Nurturing Safety TOXIC WOMB Negative emotions Attempted abortion Threat/Anxiety Metaphysical evil Paranoia Lack of safety	Cervix closed Entrapment Pressure Oppression/Compression No exit/No way out Difficulty with breath Abandonment Aloneness Depression Powerlessness/Futility Victimization	Cervix opened Biological fury Sexual arousal Pain/intensity Aggression/Murderous rage Contractions/birth struggle Clashing energies Elemental power Fight for freedom	Birth Emergence into light Obstetric interventions Union during nursing Decompression Freedom Expansion of space Cessation of danger, pain, and struggle Completion Safety

Journey or going through birth, when it's like this, is not leaving some pleasant place. We may not have a reference point for safety. And this brings to the journey a special kind of poignancy.

Now, the second reason we may not remember a sense of safety is that, even if we actually had a good womb, it could be that our birth, and our early time on the planet with our families and unique environment, might not have been safe. It may have been quite strongly the opposite, such as illness, some type of dysfunction in the family: addiction in the parents, or abuse, all kinds of reasons. And if this is the case, then in our psyches, any memory of safety we may have once had is covered up pretty strongly with the other painful memories.

But here's some good news: If we discover that this is the case with us — that is, that we can't remember a good womb or recall any other experience of safety, for that matter — we're not cursed. Because through many practices, we all have access to the collective unconscious the way Carl Jung described it. And in the collective dimension, we can definitely experience what it's like to have a good womb — to be safe and to have our needs met — because safety and a good womb are archetypes that everyone can access.

In fact, one of the major parts of healing — for those of us who have had a difficult birth or tough early history after our birth — is that once we begin to make conscious these painful experiences, and once we begin to be free of them, these archetypes of the positive aspects of the death/rebirth process and birth itself begin to be active in our lives. When this occurs, we can be sure we are well on our way down the road to healing. But it's a process, as we have been saying. It won't happen overnight. But it definitely does take place. I've seen it happen many times over the years for hundreds of seekers.

Now we should have a pretty good sense of what the Free Zone can feel like, where it comes from, and how it's an integral part of the way we all move toward wholeness. So, let's play with how it shows up in some specific scenes of well-known movies.

Test Screening — The Safe Zone

Paradise

Finding Nemo is just gorgeous to look at. Brilliant colors shimmer in the currents. I'm color blind, and it's still one of the most beautiful things I've ever seen. It's sweet too. Even though it's full of loss, fear, pain, and longing, it's still sweet. Not sugar sick sweet. But full of love. And the score by Thomas Newman perfectly accentuates the sweetness and the beauty of the images we see.

How to Listen to a Movie

For me, it's impossible to separate great movies from their musical scores. I have a tremendous passion for them. So, as I'm writing, I'm running through sound tracks in my head, and this leads me right off to Thomas Newman. I feel he's one of the greatest. Listen to the moody tracks in Road to Perdition. *And the transcendent and heart-rending work he did in* Angels in America, *as well as* The Shawshank Redemption *and the misunderstood masterpiece,* Meet Joe Black.

Ennio Morricone was another composer who made some of the most memorable movie music ever. Sergio Leone's trilogy that put Clint Eastwood on the map: A Fistful of Dollars, For a Few Dollars More, *and the classic,* The Good, the Bad, and the Ugly. *These were (what were they called?) "spaghetti Westerns." And they shattered the mold for Westerns, for later masters like Sam Peckinpah and Eastwood himself.*

I'll also never forget, being sweet sixteen, experiencing the first of these with my girlfriend. It was like, "Well, we could go see this, what the hell?" and then just getting devastated by it. It was Morricone who elevated those films into the epic category. Two of his other music masterpieces were Leone's Once Upon a Time in America, *which was awesome — the long version, not the first shortened studio release. And Brian de Palma's* Casualties of War.

At the moment, I can't recall any exceptional movie experience I've had that did not have an incredible score. Somebody pretty tapped in once said music is the language of the soul. It tends to just bypass our surface defenses and mental chatter like they're not even there. In fact a bad soundtrack can absolutely ruin a movie. Whereas a great one can transform a mediocre movie into a masterpiece, and make a turkey worth sitting through.

Every epic is notable for the track. We might not be able to recall a scene to mind too quickly, but a melody will send our souls and part the curtain again, just like that. Think of just a few of the classics: Gone with the Wind, Lawrence of Arabia, Ben Hur, Dr. Zhivago, Schindler's List, Braveheart, Rob Roy, Gladiator, The Piano, The Lord of the Rings, Titanic, The Thin Red Line. *When we do, we're not really thinking, are we? We're listening. Movie and music are one.*

The Safe Zone

Almost all of *Finding Nemo* is about being in the womb — that oceanic universe. Just about the whole thing is like an amazing adventure in the first stage of the death/rebirth process. The first part sets the stage for the on-going womb experience. It starts with love and connectedness — a married fish couple, waiting on their eggs to hatch into children. So far, so good. That's heaven. But death strikes all of a sudden — it's the end of safety — for now.

After that, the story really begins. Little Nemo prepares for his first day in school. His father — who's actually a tad annoying through the whole flick, if you ask me, but that's probably because he just triggers me somehow — is way over-protective. But it's hard to blame him. And then, at around eleven minutes in, this amazing scene happens.

All the little kindergarten fishes hop a ride on the back of a wonderful, sweet old giant manta ray. And off they go to school. It's hard to imagine how beautiful this segment is. It's only about thirty seconds long. The ray sings a sea-faring ditty as they swoop through a paradise world of plants and coral, all to the sounds of the score's sweet, heart-rending, soul-opening note. Thirty seconds, and I'm in there. The movie's got me. I'm already crying.

Welcome to the Safe Zone: the world of heaven, of connectedness, of fulfillment. This is the good womb. This is the innocence before experience, before there's even any inclination that we have to worry about such a thing as birth. Now I may not have had a whole lot of that feeling in my childhood. But when I watch that scene, it's like a tuning fork. And I'm vibrating somewhere deep inside of me. It might not have been this life, but it could have been my birth. And if it wasn't my birth, then I'm connecting with an echo from the world where we all have access to that kind of feeling — the world of archetypes — those core patterns common to us all.

So then all the little kid fishes are goofing around and swim up to the edge of the reef. And bingo, the deep dark beckons, a great vast emptiness beyond the familiar. The music's right there with it. And in this vastness looms all the possibilities of losing connection, of aloneness, and danger. It's all just potential at this point. But they look out, and there it is — a boat, a line disappearing out of sight in the deep — that thing — whatever it is. The loss of innocence, the beginning of fear. Could that be like the first contraction? Like, "Oh, hell, what's up?"

Or is this the Call to Adventure? Have you ever felt that weird mix of excitement, longing, and fear? Like when you're at the edge of a high cliff, and you get dizzy and sick with terror just looking over? But you also want to jump

— not to die, but to take a leap of faith, to really break some boundaries. That's like the Call. And sure enough, in this movie, it's the beginning of the adventure. School's about to be out. And Nemo's heading out, which sets up the story for the whole movie: finding Nemo.

So in this seemingly innocuous summertime blockbuster, made for children and their parents, are imbedded some of the deepest longings we humans have. The connectedness of family, the pain of its loss, and the fight for its return. We relate to the death/rebirth of both the child fish and the father fish — not their physical deaths, but the deaths of who they thought they were. And through the trials of the movie, the hero's journey they each go on, they are reborn into new selves. And, in the end, reunited in family connectedness. Yea!

But, you know what? It's not just the story; that kind of thing gets done all the time. It's guaranteed to be a crowd pleaser. After all, these are archetypal feelings. But what separates this one from so many others is the beauty. And such a beauty it is — of sight and sound. As I write, my heart opens even now, just to see it and hear it in my mind.

On Earth as It Is in . . . Well, Somewhere Else

Director Danny Boyle burst on the scene with *Trainspotting*, a devastating, yet hilarious, addictions story which was the breakout role for Ewen McGregor. There's one ridiculously unforgettable scene, or maybe it's seriously forgettable (I'll leave you to decide), where the main character, played by McGregor, is addicted to heroin, and he's trying to kick.

So, he's taken some kind of surrogate downer to help him get through his "jones," but then he's got the runs, so the pill passes through him and goes undigested into the toilet — gets flushed away. And when to his horror he realizes what he's done, in a heroic act of insane desperation — known only to addicts, I might add — he dives into the toilet and swims through the pipes in search of the magic pill like it's *Twenty Thousand Leagues Under the Sea*, but it's really more like this incredible voyage through the birth canal.

But that's not the scene of Danny Boyle's, or the movie, I want to talk about, even though it's spot-on death and rebirth. I'm sorry. It was just too good not to mention. But the one that's perfect for the zone we're in now comes from *The Beach*, Leonardo Di Caprio's first film after *Titanic*, which was adapted from a harrowing book by masterful writer, Alex Garland. It's one of those universal, or archetypal, tales of our search for heaven on earth. And yes, if you're beginning to see the connection between heaven and the Safe Zone, you're right on track.

So, this version of the Shangri-La epic is about three teenagers — 21st century expatriates like the generations that have gone before them, from the Sixties on back, through the Beats to the Left Bank, and on and on — who are enacting the wanderer *puer eternis* archetype, except this time on the world stage. They're the ones who follow the Ecstasy/rave scene from Goa in India to wherever it's happening. This time they've landed in Thailand, face-to-face with what B. B. King sang and played so hauntingly about three decades before, but which tells the tale of what just about every expatriate at one time or another has gone through: "The thrill is gone."

So, what happens is, this older expat type kills himself in the room next to the Di Caprio character's squalid hovel where he's passing time — depressed, burnt-out, and disillusioned. And there in the dead guy's room he finds a bloody map to an island that supposedly no one knows about, with the perfect beach — pristine, untouched — in short, it's paradise. It's the dream, the answer to all his prayers. It's the culmination, he finally understands, of the force which has been driving him and all his companions to search the world over for heaven on earth.

What he doesn't quite get yet is that it's the same thing Morpheus told Neo about in *The Matrix*, on that first stormy night as they sat in front of the fire, when he offered Neo the chance of his life — and us too, for that matter, if we could but be awake enough to hear it. Take the blue pill, and condemn ourselves to lives of mediocrity — forget all about the dreams that drive us, because they're not real anyway. Or take the red pill and let life show us just how deep the rabbit hole goes.

And that thing that gnaws us, and whose voice we can never quite seem to silence, is what Morpheus called "the splinter in your mind." What he was saying validates what we've been referring to here: which is that happiness is an inside job. By that I mean, there may be actual places in the world that are the archetypes of heaven and perfection, but it's way more likely that to find that place or thing, we've got to make some kind of change within ourselves first — pull the splinters out of our minds. Then we just may find that wherever we're standing is holy ground, is that place — and not just the dream of some greener pasture way over wherever — somewhere — some Beach where, if we can just find it in this world, everything will be perfect.

But I get ahead of myself. Because he and his two friends don't know this yet — like all of us haven't known this yet for so much of our lives — which may account, at least in part, for all the great explorations, on Earth and in the spirit

— of all the profound discoveries, the works of art, the finest aspirations of humanity to create perfection here on this planet.

But again I get ahead of myself. So, what do they do? Like any great heroes, they have many adventures. They take a boat as far as they can. And after that they swim through shark-filled waters, nearly drowning on the way. And when they finally get to the island, they crawl through snake and bug infested jungle, and flee from savage drug lords, until they accidently, or serendipitously, swim over a waterfall into a pristine pool, and meet their Guide — the one who takes them to the lost tribe. And from there, our next Free Zone scene begins.

To the music of Moby — one of the most seductive minstrels of the new generation — they walk through the dunes and the palms and get their first glimpse of the Beach. And they're right — it is heaven on earth, just as they've imagined. The camera walks with them out of the rainforest and into the sand, and we see the cove, the lagoon, in their faces before the camera reveals it: like a turquoise, sometimes cobalt, liquid jewel surrounded by a crown of towering shoals, sunlight firing the wavelets like raindrops of light.

Then, back to their faces as they collapse on the sand as though beneath velvet coverlets, taking them into Mother Earth. These are the earth's new beautiful people — young, innocent, carrying the hopes and dreams of a world gone mad. Mad except for here, for now, in a perfect purity that they imagine nothing can tarnish. Because they feel with absolute certainty that this purity is the nature of their souls.

They have returned, just as they have been driven to do their whole lives. They have felt the splinters in their minds, have done what they must do to follow the dream. And now, here they are, on the shores of perfection — so far. And just as the camera pans from the magic lagoon upwards, through time-lapse into a moon-lit, star-filled deep black night, you feel that, in some similar way, that dream will be eclipsed.

I won't tell you what happens next. But we can guess. Because we are beginning to learn that, as we've said a hundred times already — heaven is an inside job. But if heaven is an inside job, then so is hell. And if we're going to project heaven on some place outside ourselves, then we're going to project, you guessed it, that other thing too — hell.

This search for fulfillment, driven by some barely glimpsed dream, is universal. If we read any literature from any culture — poems, novels, epics, comics, whatever. If we look at any work of art — painting, sculpture, architecture.

Or listen to any music — Indian ragas, symphonies, trance, didgeridoo of Australian aboriginals, drumming of the !Kung bush people, or any great rock and roll — we can see, hear, and feel this perfection calling, this dream of heaven, the Safe Zone.

This siren call of perfection can pull us two ways. One way is forward, as though it's a lighthouse way out in front of us, drawing us toward some future apotheosis, some point omega — a Free Zone, which we can reach, once we've traversed the pain and tribulation of the Trapped Zone and the War Zone. Or, we can be pulled back, as though in a dream, a faint, ancient memory of some past perfection we have lost — almost like the Biblical Fall. Where there's a blueprint of a perfection that we knew.

We know this isn't something fanciful from our imagination, because it's a real place that we already know. We've been there. I'll use a music metaphor again. This dream of perfection that we feel is our birthright seems to exist in two different octaves — two complementary levels with the same theme.

The first, the most ancient, and the highest octave which exists in us is that of heaven, a place from which we came, a home that we once had, a perfection, a unity of father/mother god, if you will. We have an inkling that we knew and lived this perfection before we incarnated as human beings, before we took the journey of individuality. And somehow, as the myths go, we lost the reality of this perfection, yet retained the memory deep within us, like the splinter in our mind that Morpheus talked about.

Okay, that's one level. Another octave is our birth process itself, where, this time, instead of hearing the memory of a long-ago heaven inside us — maybe another dimension somewhere — we have the memory of a place like the Safe Zone — the good womb. And so all the dreams we pursue in this world, where we seem to be fighting toward something, are actually attempts at recreating our return to the womb. They spring from a longing to re-experience the safety, freedom, and perfection that we know is real, because it's a powerful memory inside us of something we actually, physically experienced.

So, there it is: *The Beach* — the symbol of every human's longing for what can be, or what has already been, the heaven and safety we would love to re-realize in our lives. And Danny Boyle and Alex Garland have nailed it — right down to the symbolism of the beach, the pristine ocean which is a perfect re-enactment of a return to the amniotic universe, the warm safe waters of our mother's womb. Perhaps we're not crazy after all to feel we know this as a physical place.

So, which is it? Are we forever moving backward, trying to repeat or recapture what we once had? Or are we struggling toward the beacon which the lighthouse flashes at us in a relentless rhythm of longing on all those cold, dark nights when we feel so lost and alone? Forward or back? Well, what if it's both? What if they are both real, and, in our search for ourselves, it's essential that we open to the call of both directions?

Like the Greek, two-headed god, Janus, facing both ways, forward and back, our past and our future, they both have something powerful to say to us. And if we ignore one or the other, we miss the fullness of perfection, the possibility of our own fulfillment right here in the present, whatever that may be.

But don't look to this book to answer that "forward or backward" question. This one can't do it, and, truth be told, I don't think any book can. Books can fire us up, though, make us want to go a'roving. Because this journey we are all on, not any book we read, holds the secret answers to all the questions we will ever ask. But if what you are reading now intrigues you in any way, then you may want to rent *The Beach* and watch it, or any one of a thousand other films. Because deep in the heart of every filmmaker is a seeker, just as deep in the heart of every movie-goer is a wayfarer too.

Trouble in Paradise

The Thin Red Line was Terrence Malick's third film, made in 1998. Before that he hadn't done a movie since the mid-seventies. The one he made then was *Days of Heaven*, and his first one was *Badlands*. Back in that day he was the new bad boy genius — kind of like Quentin Tarantino was a few years ago — with the bright star, the big future.

But after *Days of Heaven*, he disappeared. He stopped making movies because he didn't want to spend all his time fighting not to compromise his vision, which so often happens in Hollywood. Then he emerged in the late nineties with *The Thin Red Line*, which enraptured a lot of us fans. Since then he's done *The New World*, the story of Pocahontas and Captain John Smith and his ode to spirit and nature. And we Malick fans get to be ecstatic once more, this time about his *Tree of Life*.

On the surface, *The Thin Red Line* is a story about the U.S. invasion to retake the Solomon Islands from the Japanese during World War II. But at a deeper level, it's really an epic, spiritual tone poem on the nature of existence.

The Safe Zone

Some movies I just have to hang out with, or be with, like I would a poem. Some are hard to follow. But they're powerful anyway; there's no denying it. With this kind, I find that if I concentrate real hard on trying to figure out what's happening, I actually miss the real impact of the movie.

How to Eat a Movie

Terrence Malick doesn't seem to have come from the same planet as other filmmakers. There is absolutely nobody like him. People either love him or hate him. I adore him. His movies defy the traditional Hollywood party line: the three act structure, don't use voice-over too much, keep the action moving — that kind of thing. If I watch his movies with the same eyes I use in watching more everyday films, I have a hard time understanding them. Same as I don't get poetry, if I do that.

Most of the time when I read a poem, I'm lost. Unless, at least for the first read, I just let it wash over me without trying too hard. That way, I feel I get the essence of the meaning. It's like I let a different part of my consciousness than the rational intellect do the reading. Maybe it's intuition, I don't know.

But this way, I get it. Meaning just sort of emerges, or simply happens, without my trying. And then when I read it again, a different level of understanding comes to light. The same goes for movies. All of Terrence Malick's movies do this to me. This is what also happened to me, for instance, with Christopher Nolan's Memento, *the amazing movie where the hero had amnesia, and the movie began at the end and worked its way back to the beginning. And also Stephen Gaghan's* Syriana, *a powerful film about the world oil crisis with multiple complex story lines. And many more.*

Speaking of seeing a movie more than once, some people think I'm nuts because I'll go back to a movie again and again. In Denmark not too long ago, I was rhapsodizing about the Lord of the Rings *trilogy, and a friend of mine laughed and said, "Get a life." I told him this* was *my life.*

I mean, if you were wandering through a museum, and you saw an astounding painting, you wouldn't just want to see it for the few minutes you were in the gallery, would you? You'd want to be able to be with it as much as you could, because it thrills the heart, the soul, or whatever. Maybe you buy a print, or make a point to visit the museum on a regular basis. It's special when the invisible archetype of beauty, or power, or ecstasy, or whatever, manifests in this world. But when it does, we owe it to ourselves to bask in it. We deserve it. These works of art are gifts. And I am delighted to receive.

Now, many may question whether any film is great art. But I don't have to. Here's how it works for me. The first time I go to a movie, I let the movie eat me; I surrender to the experience, let myself be consumed by it. I try not to add any of what I call my secondary faculties, like judgment, criticism, analyzing — all that deconstructing crap we do with our minds. I want to stick with my primary faculties, like intuition, my senses, my soul, if you want to call it that, the part of me that is open to inspiration.

And maybe the second time, I let the movie eat me too. But the third time, and all the times after that, I start to eat the movie. That is, I become absorbed in a performance, a certain look, a piece of the score, a scene, shades of meaning. I let those pieces send my heart soaring. And then the next time, it'll be something else. If it's a wide bandwidth of experience, a big canvas, I discover that in one viewing I identify with a certain character. And in another viewing, a different character feels like me. This is what happens in our Lord of the Rings *seminar. Half way through the week, participants are reporting about their Inner Gandalf, their Inner Arwen, or the Inner Gollum. "Movie Yoga," right?*

There are a few other films that fly in the face of your average Hollywood movie, no matter where they're made. I mean, they don't fit conventional, party-line, story-telling structure. Some of the new Japanese movies are like that — those, for example by the awesome director Hayao Miyazaki, like Princess Mononoke *and* Spirited Away. *It's not that these filmmakers are just trying to do something different. It has more to do, I guess, with the Asian psyche altogether, which doesn't seem to quite put things in the every-day Western mental box — the way we're used to seeing it.*

But a non-Hollywood approach to story form is certainly not exclusive to Asian directors. Throughout movie history, creative filmmakers from all over the world have defied the conventional structures of the times. And I hope they always will. We're Movie Yogis, right? What we want to do is break free. So, their freedom to take chances gives us a better chance too to shatter the molds that have held us back. Let's hope they never stop pushing us.

Anyway, Terrence Malick's films are definitely like this. It's best to sit back, suspend the old rational left-brain, and let the experience just wash over us. Basically, quit thinking. Quit trying to get it. Come to think of it, this is a good recipe for watching all movies. We can do one of two things. Try to fit a movie through the filters of our pre-constructed headspaces. Or we can be willing to let the movie change us, be open to the mystery, and let the movie reconfigure our psyches, instead of the other way around.

There's so much beauty in *The Thin Red Line*, so much power. It's about way more than just the first stage of the death/rebirth process. But the way it opens is just a perfect example of how movies are frequently epics of death and rebirth, and so they'll begin with this first stage we've been discussing — the Safe Zone. Malick may even be one of the few who's actually doing this consciously. So, here we'll just highlight this one part of the movie's treasures, even though I'd love to go through the whole thing.

The opening shot is unforgettable: To a wave of sound — orchestra heavy on the bass, the beginning of a score by Hans Zimmer that manages to enhance the poetry without overpowering it — a crocodile slides into a fetid swamp pool and disappears. This is a perfect example of what we call the 'toxic womb'.

You see, you can think of the first zone as home, where it's supposed to be safe — love, connectedness, our needs getting met. But many times it's toxic, not safe, because of all the different types of trauma we go through. Either painful things happened to us that shouldn't have, like illness, or something should have happened, like care and support, but didn't, because of neglect. So, that's the swamp, instead of the clean, clear pool.

The crocodile is a striking symbol of darkness, danger, evil, and abuse coming in from the outside. Lots of us report going through our lives feeling a sort of non-specific anxiety or sense of danger. Well, rough childhoods can definitely account for that. But so does birth. Next, the scene shifts, and we're out of the swamp and on the edge of paradise: a primeval forest. We hear a voice-over about the struggle between the light and the dark — two forces in nature at war — and the question, "Do they vie with each other?"

That's the preamble. It sets up how paradise gets lost. But for the next twenty minutes we really are in paradise: a South Sea island village and a Shangri-La of native people. Their home is a heaven of laughter, abundance, simplicity, connectedness, love, and safety — all the elements of the good womb, the safe childhood home, and the innocence before the journey. And then into this heaven wander two army deserters. The inhabitants embrace them as innocent children would.

One of deserters is played by Jim Caviezel, who has the eyes of an angel. Malick supposedly looked far and wide for just those eyes. So did Mel Gibson when he cast him as Jesus in *The Passion of the Christ*. His character is the soul of the film. In this scene, he himself might as well be one of the original people. He is that filled with innocence and purity.

The two deserters play in the unspoiled beauty of Mother Nature. They blot out the world of war. The epic journey they're running from is forgotten for the moment. And then, they see the ship coming for them — the symbol of war, responsibility, struggle, and death. There's trouble in paradise. It's a symbol similar to the crocodile sliding into the pool. Using our birth metaphor, the contractions have begun. Soon, they will make the journey of death and, hopefully, rebirth as they fight their way across the island. But for now it's time to leave the womb.

Much later in *The Thin Red Line,* the Caviezel character returns to the island. This is after he's faced the horrors of war — the death, destruction, and disillusionment. And he finds paradise lost. It's not just a physical change, either, although there is that: run-down hovels, blackened fire pits, trash.

The end of innocence is palpable. The children scatter. Old folks peer from the shadows. Over all is a pall of gloom and emptiness. Malick has a lot of themes in the film, and this is just one of them: the loss of innocence. The tragedy of being expelled from the Garden of Eden. So much for paradise.

Paradise Shattered

As we go through these films, remember where we started from. Think back to the total beauty, innocence, and simplicity of *Finding Nemo*. The yearning in each of us to return to *The Beach*, to bask in oceanic ecstasy. And how things got a little more complicated in *The Thin Red Line*. Well, the womb, or home, can be the source of even darker memories than this. Now remember, when we say womb, and home, it doesn't have to be just our birth womb, or our growing up home. Those are just archetypal metaphors. I mean, we can have this feeling of home at the beginning of any cycle of our lives: starting a relationship, going off to school, or moving to another state or country.

And sometimes, we can be in what feels like a safe place, and then, wham! — someone close to us dies: there's illness, loss, a car accident — anything that feels like an attack or an outright violent shake-up of the peace we were feeling. There are plenty of movies that convey this kind of feeling too. Here are a couple of them.

I've already mentioned *Jaws*. That opening scene sequence is a part of film history. It fits perfectly with our perspective. Almost three minutes in, this beautiful teenager undresses, and heads for a moonlight swim, while her drunken boyfriend staggers around trying to get out of his clothes, so he can join her. It's all good times — the party on the beach with friends, the safe light of the fire, alcohol, music.

Many of us can remember what comes next, but we couldn't guess at the time how it could be so shocking. There's a piece of music by John Williams — it's been used so much it's now a caricature, full of menace and slowly escalating danger and terror. She's backstroking in the waters: the good womb. And then there's the Attack of the Century, one of the most horrifying, sickening things put on film up to that point. It's almost a blueprint, the one by which they'll all be measured. It perfectly represents the abrupt end of safety, as well as how the onset of birth can feel to the fetus like danger and an attack from the outside.

Master horror director Tobe Hooper does something very similar to this in a later film Spielberg produced, *Poltergeist*, about how a little girl becomes a conduit for scary things, which invade her home from another dimension. It's the final night of the story, one hour and forty-two minutes into the movie. And things are already seriously escalated. I mean, bad stuff is flying out of the walls and oozing up all over the place.

The dimensions to the dark side are wide open. And everybody's panicking magnificently. You'd think that would be enough. But no. Not with Hooper and Spielberg. So the half-naked leading lady (of course) slips into this half-finished swimming pool — at night, during a thunderstorm. Into the black waters, bounded by the slick, black, muddy walls.

Sounds like the prelude to some of our worst fears, right? Then all these skeletons and half-rotted corpses bubble up around her. And she gets all tangled up in them as she tries to claw her way up the muddy banks. But all the time she's sliding right back into the bony arms of the dead. This is another perfect example of the toxic womb.

If we are experiencing this, it feels like the Safe Zone has become the Unsafe Zone. It signals that, even though the unknown ahead of us — birth — might be scary, it's probably better than where we are now. This brings to mind one of the great one-liners from some recovering addict: "The way I got to heaven was by backing out of hell."

CHAPTER 9
THE TRAPPED ZONE

If Aragorn survives this war, you will still be parted. If Sauron is defeated and Aragorn becomes King, and all that you hope for comes true, you will still have to taste the bitterness of mortality. Either by the sword or the slow decay of time, Aragorn will die, and there will be no comfort for you — no comfort to ease the pain of his passing. He will come to death: an image of the splendor of kings in glory undimmed before the breaking of the world. But you, my daughter, you will linger on in darkness and in doubt, as night falling in winter comes without a star. Here you will dwell, bound to your grief, under the fading trees, until all the world is changed and the long years of your life are utterly spent. Arwen, there is nothing for you here, only death.

~ Elrond, lord of Rivendel to his daughter Arwen,
The elf maiden: *Lord of the Rings: The Two Towers*

Proximo, to Maximus: *We mortals are but shadows and dust.*

~ *Gladiator*

Phil: *You want a prediction about the weather, you're asking the wrong Phil. I'll give you a winter prediction: It's gonna be cold; it's gonna be grey. And it's gonna last you the rest of your life.*

~ *Groundhog Day*

Pee Wee Herman: *It's like you're unraveling a big, cable-knit sweater that someone keeps knitting and knitting and knitting and knitting and knitting and knitting.*

~ *Pee Wee's Big Adventure*

The Trapped Zone

> Miriam: *As the sound of the playgrounds faded, the despair set in. Very odd, what happens in a world without children's voices.*
>
> ~ *Children of Men*

If the Safe Zone can be felt as heaven and connectedness, then the Trapped Zone could be compared to hell. And if you're coming from a toxic womb hell in the Not-Safe Zone, then the second phase, the Trapped Zone, is just a deeper hell. When the birth process or the journey begins (remember the two levels we can experience), we can feel as though we are being cast out of heaven. We can suddenly feel alone, empty, powerless, depressed, shamed, full of low self-esteem — the opposite of what we were feeling before.

Sometimes the way we interpret this is that, because we're no longer in a safe place, we must have deserved getting cast out. We feel that it's our fault. The other possible thing we feel is that we are victims. The Trapped Zone is a core level of this pervasive feeling we all go through. In any event, now we are truly on our own.

If we're focusing on just the biological birth, then there's another whole level of pain that's experienced. Because, in the Trapped Zone, the fetus is really stuck. It can't move forward. There's no way out of the womb yet, because the cervix is still closed. There's no light at the end of the tunnel.

Going into the Trapped Zone can feel like a trip down to hell — to darkness, total aloneness, and the sudden arising of the fear of approaching death. In the Hero's Journey metaphor, it's the time when we cross the threshold into an alternate universe, where everything gets turned upside down, and we're full of confusion, fear, and hopelessness.

This place is the "life sucks and then you die" planet. The "life is nothing but a veil of tears" type of world. You think, "What's the use?" Time seems to stop. It's as though, "I'm here now. I've always been here, and I always will be." It's kind of a Fellini planet: the merry-go-round that never ends, in the sick, twisted carnival of puppets and clowns. I don't think I've ever met anybody who didn't know this world, at least during some time in their lives. In the workshops I give, the participants are all just nodding their heads right about now, as if to say, "No kidding, we know that one."

The Trapped Zone — Test Screening

No Exit

When the Call comes, we have to answer. When the walls of the uterus contract, it's leaving time — one way or the other. Brings a whole new meaning to 'kicking and screaming', doesn't it? At this stage in the journey, we're apt to be thinking two things at the same time. One, somewhere down deep is a tickle in the gut, a heart flutter, that to get born, we'll have to make a decision to die. That's because birth is often a life-threatening situation. It sure is, at least, a life-changing one. And two, what makes it confusing is that another part of us thinks we ought to be able to just skip on down the Yellow Brick Road — no big deal. But it's just not that simple.

Whether it's a Hero's Journey or biological birth, we find ourselves caught in the middle of two opposing forces. One compels us to power through. And the other stands dead in our way. It can hit us at the emotional level, like feeling incredibly stuck in our lives. But it can also be seriously physical — an intense pressure coming from everywhere, closing in. Like there's a ten ton weight on our chest. We can't get our breath. There's a vise around our head, neck, and shoulders. George Lucas gave us an experience of this space way back in the late seventies.

It was a long time ago, in a galaxy far, far away, in the middle of a galactic military confrontation — *Star Wars*, I believe they called it. You remember when our heroes first got caught on the Death Star? There was a firefight, and Luke, Han, Princess Leia, and Chewy all dove into a giant trash bin. It was shades of that swimming pool in *Poltergeist* again — dark spooky water full of unidentifiable trash. After they trade a few signature potshots at each other about whose fault it is, they see a ripple in the water. A scaly back slips out of the filth and disappears again.

Now, so far, doesn't this sound a little familiar? If you think we've been here before, you'd be right. It's the toxic womb — anxiety, danger, the unknown coming in from the outside. A creepy eye emerges and checks them out. Next thing you know, Luke goes under. That thing's got him! Definitely a rough beginning. But just when we think it's all over for the kid, he pops up. Yay!

But uh oh, what's that sound? Some kind of ominous grinding. And then, the walls start closing in. Our heroes do what they can to brace them, but it's no use. It's not just a trash bin; now it's a trash compactor. It's not just a toxic womb. It's a dangerous birth canal closing in around us. It gets smaller and smaller. There's no way out. They're totally stuck, no more options, nowhere to go. They're powerless to help themselves. It's all futile, over, the end. The pressure builds to the bursting point, or should I say, to the "squshing" point.

But, wait a minute. We're only half-way through the first of what ends up being six movies. So they can't all die now. Sure enough, the droids, R2D2 and C3PO, rescue them. Yippee! First time I saw it, no kidding, all of us — and the theater was packed — breathed a big sigh of relief. Not because they didn't die, because we all knew there was a lot of movie left. George wasn't going to kill off the heroes just yet. But the sigh was because in our own ways, we also all know that kind of tension in our lives and probably, unconsciously, in our births. We've been through what it's like to have no options: to be stuck, to be powerless, to feel everything closing in on us.

Now Lucas did it in a funny way, so it was a method of describing a horrible situation in a way people could handle it, in a PG kind of way. And our friend Spielberg did it too in *Indiana Jones and the Temple of Doom*. Except then, Indiana and his buddy were on the wrong side of a sliding door studded with steel spikes that was about to skewer them. But the feelings it brings up in us are not really funny. In fact they're pretty R rated. And we experience them all the time in the movies.

When I was little, I saw a movie about Jack the Ripper. The whole thing was in black and white, except for one shot. It was when the Jack character got caught in an elevator shaft, and the elevator car was coming down on him, and he knew he was going to be "squashed". So, the camera point-of-view is in the elevator looking down at the floor when Jack gets crushed. And the only thing in color in the entire flick was his blood and guts squishing up through the floorboards.

How did I get into that movie? I, a mere baby. Just lucky, I guess. It was way before ratings, by the way. But my point is, this kind of tension runs through many movies. Every prison flick — *The Great Escape, The Shawshank Redemption, Cool Hand Luke*, the television show, *Oz*. Every great insane asylum movie — *One Flew Over the Cuckoo's Nest*, and many more — they all trigger that awful edgy, panicky thing. Because we all know it: one way or the other, what it's like to be physically, emotionally, or mentally trapped.

What makes it so bad is, in just about every case, we have all had at least a taste of freedom from somewhere before, maybe even the memory of the good womb. And we'd all sure like to go back, right? But guess what? That's not going to happen. No way around it. We've got to power through, even if the walls keep closing in more and more. It basically just plain sucks.

In Search of the Blue Fairy

Feeling connected, "a part of," as the word "yoga" means, or having some kind of bedrock belief that we have a home base, tends to make even the darkest times just a little brighter. That is, it does if we can find some kind of internal link to it, a memory of it, like the good womb we've discussed, and oneness with the mother. But when birth starts, and we're ripped from the womb, or metaphorically from the arms of the mother, cast out of heaven or torn from safety, sometimes we can't remember or reconnect with that good thing. All we seem to have is that wound of aloneness. And we can all relate to that. Because who among us has not had many of these moments, or at least a few? I mean, in every soul journey we make, there's a big part of it we have to do alone.

So, we're going to see this aloneness in films, because it's archetypal to us all. And because not just us, but the filmmakers too are dealing with it. And it won't always be done in a humorous way either, like in *Star Wars*. Sometimes, it's just absolutely straight: the raw, naked truth of the pain.

Gut Checks

So, what's a 'gut check'? A gut check is a cheap shot in a movie, a manipulative short cut to get moviegoers to have a big reaction. In comedies, this would be overused slapstick and just throwing in a fart joke when they can't come up with anything funnier. In horror, it's having something go "Boo!" all the time as a substitute for serious psychic dread. And in dramas it'd be something like what happened in Terms of Endearment.

Now I loved that movie. It was just cruising, tearing me up all the way. I was in there. And then the Debra Winger character gets cancer and dies. I'm sorry, that's a gut check. I mean, the movie was way intense enough already — they'd done that thing. They'd more than pulled it off. But kill off a loveable character, and that's the cheapest, easiest way to jerk up a few extra tears and get a guaranteed audience reaction. I just didn't think it was necessary. It basically just pissed me off.

So, okay, it activated me. But you know, I was already triggered. The death thing ended up just distracting me from the rest of my catharsis. Ultimately,

The Trapped Zone

> *after I finish getting triggered, I welcome in movies the "raw, naked truth of the pain," as I said in the main text. And why not? Especially if I'm doing Movie Yoga. Let the movie eat me, so I can heal, right? But, no doubt, it can be a real walk on the wild side.* Terms of Endearment *definitely ate me. Okay, you're right. "Opportunity to heal! Opportunity to heal!" Don't rub it in.*

Take for example, Spielberg's *AI: Artificial Intelligence*. *AI* is basically a Pinocchio story: the epic adventure of an artificial boy fighting to become real. And one of the major themes through the whole movie was separation from the mother: the Trapped Zone of the Death/Rebirth Matrix we've been journeying through. So, cue it up — three minutes and eight seconds into Chapter 13 — get out two boxes of tissue and grab the hand of somebody you trust. Like Cipher told Neo in *The Matrix*, just before Neo found out his whole life was a lie, "It means buckle your seatbelt, Dorothy, because Kansas is going bye-bye."

Before that *AI* scene, something diabolical happens in the movie. A couple has bought a robot child, David, because their real child is in a coma. So, once they decide they're going to keep the robot, they program it indelibly, absolutely irrevocably, to completely adore its new mother. Once that happens, it can't be undone. It's emotional for me just to write about it. Why? Because this is what happens to every baby in the world. We are each hard-wired to love our mother. That's why that relationship can be such a tragedy. Because, as we all know, we can have all kinds of experiences that negate the power of that first original bond. And then we're all left with the hard-wiring plus the loss. That's what I mean by diabolical.

Back to the movie: Against all odds, their real child wakes up, and he's a bit of a demon, jealous and sneaky and all. So, this real kid orchestrates these scenarios that make David look bad to the point where the parents decide they have to take David back to the factory to be terminated. So the day comes, and the two of them, Dave and his Mom, head off to the factory.

Now, you just can't imagine the perfect love David has for his mother. I'm talking unadulterated trust. David is just adorably happy. He thinks they're going on a picnic. And the mom is really torn, because she still loves David, and is feeling enormous guilt and ambivalence about terminating him. Just before she gets to the factory, she has a half change of heart and swerves off onto a side trail. She can't bear to terminate him, so instead she decides to leave him. So, David runs innocently into the woods, ready for a special day alone with his Mom.

Then she devastates him: she tells him she's going to leave him there. And David still doesn't get it, because he's so programmed to totally trust her. "Is it a game?" he asks. But then the truth begins to dawn. His pain is absolutely heart-rending.

His mom tears herself away. "I'm sorry I didn't tell you about the world," she weeps. Is that not the refrain just about every person born on this planet hears sooner or later? To borrow a phrase from Buckminster Fuller: we have no operation manual for spaceship earth. We have no clue to the pain and the aloneness we will probably feel at one time or another.

When she pulls away, and we see David in the rearview mirror standing alone in the middle of the road, it's a perfect moment. Now, it may be perfectly horrible. But it's perfect nonetheless. It's like a crystal, it's so sharp and clear. Spielberg nailed that feeling of abandonment, loss, and aloneness. Sometimes I wonder, how did he do that? I don't know about his childhood. But regardless, he totally tapped the archetype.

In my opinion, this sense of the lost child looking to find herself or himself has never been evoked so poignantly as right here in this scene. After he gets abandoned, David ends up in a futuristic Vegas-type fun-town where he becomes obsessed with a neon blue fairy. So, just like Pinocchio, he goes in search of the Blue Fairy to see if she can make him into a real boy. He blames himself, you see, for his mother not loving him. And he believes if he can become real, then everything will be made right. How many of us have done our own version of this ritual, in order to heal that original wound and feel good about ourselves?

The Road to Hell

Remember, if the Safe Zone of death and rebirth is like heaven, then the second stage, the Trapped Zone, is definitely hell. We can feel as though we've been cast out of some protected place and thrown into its opposite, not just unsafe, but dark and terrible, too. So, frequently, the Trapped Zone is represented by a descent into the underworld.

The Shamanic Initiation

It's interesting as well that death and rebirth are also a part of shamanism — one of the oldest transformational practices on the planet. No telling how long it's been around, maybe sixty thousand years, maybe longer. It's very popular today, all over the world. One of the ways young apprentices become shamans

The Trapped Zone

is that they must go through the death/rebirth process themselves. Once they've done this — died to some old dysfunctional part of themselves and been reborn into a new, more whole sense of self — then they are able to call themselves shamans and assist in others' healing and transformation.

Shamans report frequently a descent into the underworld where they have to face demons and be dismembered and eaten by monsters. Once they've gone through this death, they ascend into the upper world on the back of an eagle, or climb the World Tree, or come out of the underworld through some other means. And that's the rebirth. We see in movies this Crossing of the Threshold, as they say in the Hero's Journey. And of course, as a part of the climax of the movie, there'll be the ascent into a heaven world, or some form of a better place.

I want to go to one particular scene that describes this journey down to hell perfectly. It has many of the elements we've been talking about in the Trapped Zone. It's not the greatest film. It's good. But it has some striking sequences, and this one never fails to trigger the participants in our groups. The film is *Jacob's Ladder*, by Adrian Lynn. It's about a Vietnam war vet — Tim Robbins plays him — who thinks he's going crazy. Turns out he was part of some drug experiment during the war, and he's having flashbacks. Anyway, we're at Chapter 27 on the DVD, about one hour and fifteen minutes in. In this scene, he just got hit by a car, and he's in the hospital. So they're wheeling him down to x-ray. And he's just looking up, eyes wide, scared and in pain, and he has a vivid flashback.

First everything's normal. Then it begins to get a little darker. And an ominous, low, rumbling sound emerges. And all of a sudden he realizes he's descending into a hellish nightmare world full of horrifying sights and sounds. At first he sees a relative's smashed bicycle — a painful memory for him. And then he's in an insane asylum. The one out of our worst nightmares. Grotesque people appear, drooling, deformed, smashing their heads against a wire wall; there's a mad woman nursing a baby, others moaning and chanting gibberish, their eyes rolling. You get the picture.

But that's just the easy part. Although we don't see him going down steps or an elevator, the effect is that he keeps going down and down. Only now the white tile floor is covered in blood, and there's nothing but wailing and screaming. And pretty soon he's bumping over body parts and guts, and passing heaps of mangled, half humanoid forms. Finally, he disappears around a corner past some monstrous, sado-masochistic, chained-up guy whose head is going wild. Now this is a pretty good representation of hell, don't you think?

I have to admit, this one's tough. But there's a method in our madness, I promise. We're not tossing this one into the mix just for shock value, although it does have that. The reason we're doing it is because the images in the scene, so spot-on, evoke core powerful feelings and memories that are associated with the Trapped Zone. First of all, there's the feeling of being stuck or trapped. And as we mentioned earlier, one of the classic situations of being trapped would be to be locked away in an insane asylum.

Okay. But why insane asylum? Because there's a stage of the journey, when we are in the death phase, but have not yet been reborn, where we can feel like we're going crazy. This is because our old way of thinking is being torn from us. We are losing our moorings. We grasp for reason, for understanding, but it's not yet there. It will be, but that's down the road. For now, we're like the Hanged Man card of the tarot deck — where everything is turned upside down. So put together feeling crazy and being trapped, and what you get is an insane asylum. Ever had a nightmare where you were in one and couldn't get out? It's like heaven to wake up from one of those dreams, because it's hell inside there, right?

So, what about the blood and the body parts? For one, the birth process can be so physically traumatic, that when we relive it, it feels like our bodies are being torn apart. At another octave, these are symbolic images of our impending death. Remember, even though the death is psychological and spiritual, it can feel like our body's actually dying too. And, as we mentioned in one of the side bars, one of the ways death can occur for us is the way it happens in the shamanic tradition — dismemberment. There are also all kinds of myths with this theme. It happened to Osiris in Egyptian myth and to Orpheus and Dionysus in Greek myth. It's a common archetype.

So, when a filmmaker puts this kind of thing in a movie, it elevates the power of the film from the personal to the archetypal level as well. It's not likely that Lynn was only going for the gross-out, though even if he was, he nailed it. Remember, a lot of what ends up on screen comes from the unconscious of the filmmaker, and that's one of the main reasons it has such power for us. It's not just his unconscious; it's ours as well.

To Be a Slave

There's an incredible sequence from one of the great silent films, *Metropolis*, directed by Fritz Lang, that demonstrates an especially clear nuance of this second stage of death and rebirth, the Trapped Zone. In these scenes, our hero discovers the vast underground machinery complex that powers Metropolis. The stark, black and white images, mostly simple geometrical shapes, make sheer visual poetry, even though it's also an image of an underworld. It's a maze of complicated gears, wheels, boilers, and levers belching fire and steam.

And swarming all over them are these human laborers, like ants or worker bees. The workers are caught in the never-ending cycle of pulling levers, adjusting dials, and keeping the precarious balance of complex cogs and gears from going haywire. They're slaves to the machines. It's as if the machines run, not with any outside purpose (like to keep the city going) but just to satisfy themselves. The humans have no purpose or existence other than to be an extension of the machines. Hmm. Sound a little too familiar? Like much of the drudgery and hum-drum of everyday survival on planet Earth?

Our hero is horrified. It's a wake-up call. He's fresh from the surface, where everything is beautiful and anesthetized, unsullied by the grime and sweat down below. Now he sees the truth. Suddenly a gauge registers a big temperature rise. Smoke, fire, and steam belch from boilers. A panicked worker tries to control the rising temperature. He's like that character on the old Ed Sullivan show who desperately struggles to keep all the plates spinning, except here it's not funny. But the gauge is out of control. He does all he can, but it's not enough. A machine explodes, and the whole complex begins to come apart. Workers fall from scaffolds into fiery vats and are boiled to death. It's becoming an inferno.

At this point, out of the chaos, an amazing image emerges. The machinery morphs into a wide-open, toothed mouth full of flames. And all of a sudden the workers become a hypnotized procession of slaves ascending the stairs in front of the great mouth. When they reach the gaping maw, they drop into its throat and disappear. The caption at the bottom reads the word spoken by our hero: "Moloch!" And the workers continue their funeral procession into the horrible mouth, where they are consumed.

Now, what's amazing is that Moloch was a bloodthirsty god of Carthage, a North African city-state made famous for its wars with Rome. You might recollect that Hannibal was a Carthaginian. Anyway, it was the custom in Carthage to sacrifice live babies to Moloch to ensure the well-being of the tribe. So think about it: sacrificing babies? Isn't that what the Trapped Zone is a metaphor for? Remember, many of us were taken care of, at home or in the womb, but then, we were cast out by the physical birth process, or by the Call of the Hero's Journey. So, for the fetus, or for the adventurer, it can feel like we are being sacrificed or thrown to the wolves, that our safety is up for grabs, and that we are on our own.

But there's another huge piece to this Moloch thing. Have you ever felt in your life — in your job, your relationship, or wherever — that everything's just one long, never-ending piece of drudgework? That it's like being on a mill wheel, turning round and round, going nowhere? That everything's futile? Like, what's the use? Why struggle? Because no matter what I do, I'll end up right back in the same place? That somehow we are slaves to a meaningless process whose only purpose is to consume our energies?

Well, this is what it was like beneath Metropolis, the vision our hero saw. And when the whole monstrous scene turned into Moloch getting fed by the slaves, couldn't we just recognize a bit of that from our own lives? Because there's a stage where it feels like we too are sacrificing ourselves to some nameless mass of machinery, a soulless system whose only purpose is to consume us. And until we wake up, we march like slaves right into the mouth of the demon god every day of our lives.

What we desperately want is to get off the tread-mill. And that's one of the main reasons why we all attempt to transform ourselves: to escape this feeling, to free ourselves. This is what the death/rebirth journey is all about. But in this Moloch stage, it's just plain hell. There is no light at the end of the tunnel. It feels like we'll be here forever, caught on the endless wheel.

There's a moment that comes to mind from near the end of *Bladerunner*, the brilliant and formula-shattering film from Ridley Scott we talked about way back in the beginning. Roy Battie, played by Rutger Hauer, is a super "replicant," or android, whose life span is going to run out any second, and he knows it. He holds the bladerunner, or bounty hunter, Deckard, played by Harrison Ford, the one who's supposed to "air him out," over the rooftop edge of a slummed-out building in the middle of an eternal rain. He can either drop him, or pull him up. And Roy says to Deckard, "Painful to live in fear, isn't it? That's what it means to be a slave."

Roy is one hundred percent right. It's a killer to live in fear. And it keeps us in slavery. Like it says in the *Big Book* of Alcoholics Anonymous, we're all driven by a hundred forms of fear. And one of the worst is to be stuck in some hell of never-ending drudgery, hopelessness, and futility. Yet one of the best reasons to go through death and rebirth is that it can free us from at least a few of these hundred forms of fear. And some of these may be the deepest, like fear of death itself. Wouldn't that be a wonderful thing?

In the Trapped Zone, our experience is that there's no way out. It can feel like this is the Big Picture, the One True Reality, that this is all that is or ever will be. But as we've said before, it's just one of the planets we've traveled to, with parameters like the hopelessness we see in *Metropolis*. There are other planets too. And until we can get to them, sometimes we just have to hole up. Circle the wagons, and wait and see. But something else is coming. I can feel it. Can't you? What's that light, way down there at the end of the tunnel?

Soon You'll Be Eaten

I wasn't going to write about Peter Jackson's *Lord of the Rings* trilogy — at least not in this book. It's so close to my soul that I want to do a whole other book on the power of these movies. And I still will. But I can't resist. So I have to say that from 1982 until *The Fellowship of the Ring* came out, there was one thing I could always count on. This was what my favorite movie of all time was and would always be: *Bladerunner*. Well, I do big talk about letting myself get shattered. And that's what *The Fellowship of the Ring* did: made me walk that big talk, and replaced my number one film.

When *Fellowship* was over, and I somehow made my way out of the theater, and after I had quit crying from the sheer ecstasy of such beauty and power, I experienced what I thought I never would again: a new favorite movie of all time. Which has now become my three favorites of all time — *The Lord of the Rings* trilogy. I can in all truthfulness say that after seeing these movies, my highest movie-going aspirations have been fulfilled.

It does not ever, ever, have to get better than this. I'm not saying it won't. In fact, lightning's going to strike me twice. It's actually about to get better, or just as perfect: Peter Jackson is producing two more Tolkien films, *The Hobbit* and another transition film to *The Lord of the Rings* trilogy. The second one has material from Tolkien's masterpiece, *The Silmarillion*. This is so perfect: Peter and his partner Phillipa Boyens are writing them. They wrote the other three. And you won't believe who's going to direct: Guillermo del Toro, the genius who did *Pan's Labyrinth* and the *Hellboy* series. He's perfect — probably the only one who could pull off replacing Peter Jackson.

But even if I wasn't about to be ascending into movie heaven again, I'm still not needing one thing else, as far as movies go. I have such gratitude to be able to feel this. It's as though I've had the chance to transcend — if only in one small area and for one time in my life — my age-old human dilemma of wanting more and more and more of whatever it is, forever. Now that's a gift.

And while we're on the subject, I just have to say one more thing. I read the *LOTR* trilogy in prep school, and the books changed my life. I've read them a number of times since, and many scenes are indelibly imprinted in my soul. I can feel, smell, see, and taste what happens, as though I am there, an actual part of the story myself. These imprints are crystal clear; they live in my psyche, more powerfully than many memories.

And when I saw the movies, I had a revelation, a peak experience. There were scenes in those films that were exactly, and I mean exactly, the way they were branded in my consciousness from reading the books. Don't ask me how this happens. It's just another part of that wondrous mystery that is, in general, the story of transformation. But it reflects also specifically something altogether astonishing about Movie Yoga. But hey, somebody stop me.

Middle Earth to Tav: *We're Here in the Trapped Zone...*

It's *The Return of the King*. Gollum's plan is unfolding exquisitely: he's manipulated Frodo into thinking Sam ate all the lembus bread, their magical elfin food. Frodo's sent Sam packing. And Frodo and Gollum have climbed the rest of the treacherous mountain stairs and entered a tunnel that Gollum says is a secret passageway into Mordor. Frodo's so trusting, plus his consciousness is being twisted by the Ring, so he doesn't have a clue what's going on. But we do.

At the end of *The Two Towers*, Gollum's talking to himself, like he does, and he's just felt betrayed by Frodo, which, in a heart-breaking way, he was, one of those tragic unstoppable twists of fate. So, he's planning a way to accomplish two goals: one, get the Ring back — always number one — and two, kill Sam and Frodo. He's thinking, and then, light bulb, he gets it: "SHE could do it, oh yes." And if you read the books, you know who SHE is. And if you haven't, are you ever about to find out.

SHE — one of the great monsters of all literature and film: Shelob, the grotesque giant spider who crawls the tunnels under the mountains on the way into Mordor, sipping the blood of orcs, elves, and humans, "having a bit o' fun," as one orc says, and finally eating what's left of all her victims. And after Gollum engineers the banishment of Sam, it's into Shelob's lair that he leads the unsuspecting Frodo. Thus beginneth our scene, where we are confronted dead-on with the chilling perfection of the Trapped Zone. Right off, we're in the birth canal, the cave through the mountain, the tunnel. The tunnel is always an archetype of initiation, of perilous adventure, of the dark journey that must be undertaken, the trials that must be faced.

The Trapped Zone

By the way, next time you see the trilogy, of the ten thousand beautiful details that could strike your heart and fancy, this time, pay attention to this one thing: in *The Fellowship of the Ring*, when we first see Frodo, he's relaxing under a tree in the Shire, that total perfection of the Safe Zone — the good womb. Frodo's chewing a piece of grass when he hears the wizard Gandalf singing. He sits up: a peaceful, carefree, gentle, sweet, happy beauty is in his face — such shining eyes and bright smile. And now, track the looks on his face as the three movies progress, to use a film term: his character arc. It's a marvel.

No way to do this right here, unless we chronicle all the changes Frodo goes through as he carries the Ring toward Mount Doom. One look would be like the haunted, heartbreaking tears after his beloved Gandalf falls into shadow, another victim of the Balrog. And then, here under the mountain, as Gollum sets him up, and the horror of what he's gotten himself into dawns on him, there comes the sickening stench of Shelob's lair circling like a nightmare incense. Oh, and one more look we'll see later, in another Zone... but now's not the time.

But here, Frodo's eyes dart from one hellish image to another as his doom dawns upon him. Bones crack and rotting flesh squishes underfoot. Animal mummies and sticky, half-rotten human cocoons twist and swing in the shadows like morgue chandeliers. And then he gets it — what Gollum has pulled off — the trick.

"Oh, Sam" is all he says, but it's too late. Sam is gone, sent away, rejected by him. His most loyal friend, the one who would die for him, trade places with him, anytime, anywhere — gone. Frodo's alone — no friends, no safety, no hope. Facing the greatest evil of his life, and almost certain death at the hands of he knows not what, yet.

But all too soon he does know, as Shelob skitters out of the black and looms above him, the monster of his worst nightmare. And what Frodo's confronted with is our worst nightmare too: the tunnel of our own deepest trials and initiations, cast out of heaven, out of safety, sent down to hell, trapped by our depression, powerlessness, and fear. All that is dangerous, life-threatening, horrifying, and torturous is personified in the dark monster of our imagination, in this case the giant spider.

Why a spider? Because they are venomous, death-dealing, and just plain creepy. Because they can trap us, as though we were as helpless as a moth. Remember, after all, this is the Trapped Zone — use the lure of their silk, to wrap us, bind us until we are unmoving, paralyzed, and total victims whose lives could be sucked from us at will. They, and monsters like them, haunt almost all our worst dreams. They haunt our births — the death-dealing forces of the canal. They represent the nameless forces of darkness that are overwhelming, always waiting in the shadows of our imagination to leap out and devour us, our dreams, our hopes, our very souls.

Shelob rushes at him as he flees, panicked, deeper into the tunnel. He loses himself more and more with every step. The more lost he gets, the more familiar all this is to her. She toys with him, takes her time. He stumbles blindly over bones and bodies until, like some fear-crazed animal, he's herded right into her thickest web. He's stuck. He beats his arms like a doomed summer moth. His struggle only makes it worse. Finally he can't move.

This is the essence of the Trapped Zone: to be stuck, completely, with no way out. Alone: to be the perfect victim. To become food for a monster. To be overtaken by all that's grotesque in our mad dreams. To be overwhelmed by darkness and lose both the memory and the hope that there was ever such a place as the Safe Zone, or will ever be one called the Free Zone. This is Frodo in the tunnel on the way to Mordor: helpless, forgotten, and lost.

But Frodo is a hero; all of us are heroes. And in our moments of greatest loss, when we have surrendered to the inevitability of our doom, our death, then each of us must find a way to pull our blades, as Frodo does. He has Sting, the magic sword whose blade glows blue when orcs are near, and as Bilbo tells him, "Made by the elves, you know." And with our swords of destiny, whatever they may be, whatever is the symbol of our summoning of the last ounce of strength and will we possess, we begin to cut ourselves free... or not. And this is where we will end this part of the tale. Because a little bit of mystery goes a long, long way. And even Spoiler Alerts can't salve the wounds of too much movie knowledge. If you haven't already, just go see it.

CHAPTER 10: THE WAR ZONE

Tony Montana: *Me, I want what's coming to me.*
Manny: *Oh, well, what's coming to you?"*
Tony Montana: *The world, chico, and everything in it.*

~ *Scarface*

Swan: *We have to convince the little housewife out there that the tomato that ate the family pet is not dangerous.*

~ *Attack of the Killer Tomatoes*

Paul Gallier: *Every time it happens, you tell yourself it's love. . .but it isn't. It's blood.*

~ *Cat People*

El Mariachi: *It's easier to pull the trigger than it is to play the guitar. Easier to destroy than create.*

~ *Desperado*

Anonymous: *I fear the only way to stop those possessed by the spirits of the book is through the act of bodily dismemberment.*

~ *Evil Dead*

Hannibal Lecter: *On a serious note I must confess I'm giving very serious thought to eating your wife.*

~ *Hannibal*

King Xerxes: *Your Athenian rivals will kneel at your feet if you will but kneel at mine.*

King Leonidas: *You are generous as you are divine, oh king of kings. Such an offer only a madman would refuse. But the, uh, the idea of kneeling, it's — you see, slaughtering all those men of yours has, uh, well it's left a nasty cramp in my leg, so kneeling will be hard for me.*

~ *300*

Marv: *This is blood for blood and by the gallon. These are the old days, the bad days, the all-or-nothing days. They're back! There's no choice left. And I'm ready for war.*

~ *Sin City*

Hang on. Even though the Trapped Zone feels like it's going to last forever, change is on the way. Everything shifts big-time in the War Zone. Biologically, what happens is the mother's cervix opens, making progress possible. Metaphorically, it means there's a light at the end of the tunnel. There's a way out of this hell. Contractions are coming on, and the fetus is struggling through the canal, and we're fighting our way down the road of our adventure. Finally, after the hopelessness of the second stage, at least now there's hope — hope that comes in a slightly more, shall we say, energetic form. There's a major struggle up ahead. But there's another plus. Where there was powerlessness, now, we've got power.

Let's put it this way: Depression gets transformed into aggression, whatever it takes to get through. In the War Zone, we confront a whole new set of intense passions. We often feel this as the great epic struggles of battle, violence, and murderous rage. It's also the zone of powerful sexual cravings and experiences. This is the world of the demonic, and elemental, volcanic power. In the Hero's Journey, it corresponds to the titanic struggle to reach the goal, to face the Supreme Ordeal, whatever that may be.

Addiction and the Zones

Just to get you thinking: If we study the different personalities of addicts, their life styles and their drugs of choice, we'll find that they tend to fall into either one of two zones we've been discussing: the Trapped Zone or the War Zone. Those who identify with the Trapped Zone gravitate toward downers: opiates (like heroin, OxyContin, and Vicodin), barbiturates, and tranquilizers. I've heard many say what they really want is to return to some place gentle —

> no struggles or worries, where their needs are always going to be met. You got it? The Safe Zone.
>
> Those who feel more comfortable with, or feel more at home on the third planet, the War Zone, seem to be attracted to stimulants, speed, and cocaine. You'll hear them speak in metaphors such as "breaking through," "going over the top," all of which correspond to getting through the War Zone into what comes next — the Free Zone. Some addicts want to go back. Others want to go forward. And the types of drugs they choose tend to reflect these particular psychological and spiritual yearnings. Worth thinking about if you're a recovering addict or an addictions therapist.

Test Screening — The War Zone

Breaking On Through to the Other Side

Often those of us who have felt hurt get stuck in the role of a victim. It's natural. It's a feature of the Trapped Zone. We may feel powerless to change our lives. But sometimes, through support from the outside, like therapy, or through a spontaneous transformation from the inside, we 'come into our power'. In order for this to happen, it can take a serious wake-up call — opening to a reservoir of energy we didn't know we had. This energy may, in the beginning, feel like anger. So, the depression of the Trapped Zone turns into the aggression of the War Zone, the power to push us through the birth canal, or down the road toward the Supreme Ordeal of the Hero's Journey: birth, or rebirth.

Aggression and testosterone: every country's 'Hollywood' is full of it. What do they say is that target population of moviegoers? Males between the ages of sixteen and twenty-six? Something like that. Young guys, and lots of old ones too, want to see things go Boom! One reason the third stage of death/rebirth, the War Zone, is so popular is just plain excitement — the adrenalin rush. It sells a lot of tickets. In the middle fifties, there was this big interest, though, in the Trapped Zone. You know, the "life is a veil of struggle and tears" phase. Great directors like Ingmar Bergman made incredible existential flicks. But, it's mostly different now. By and large, movies are a lot noisier today.

So we could close our eyes in any DVD store, pick a flick, and it could very well be a War Zone movie, because there're just so many of them. And there are a lot of good ones too. So, let's have a look at a few and see what makes them so special. And why they're such good examples of the part of the process where there's light at the end of the tunnel, but it's no walk through the park to get there.

Looks

In the main text I keep asking you to "have a look." This reminds me of something. A look. My movie consciousness is filled with special looks. Movies through the years and characters in certain scenes. And that look, the one the heart leaps to, that sears itself forever into our psyches. The one that I'll buy as a DVD, or BD now, of course, just to see over and over again. Obviously your favorite looks won't be mine. But here's a couple I won't forget:

There's a classic film from my second favorite director of all time, Michael Mann — Thief — from 1981. The main character, played by James Caan, is, you guessed it, a thief. He's just pulled off an impossible diamond heist — had to use a special blowtorch on some impregnable vault. He's in. He's out. He pulls up a chair while his crew bags the diamonds.

He pushes back his welding helmet, lights up, takes a hit, and lets the smoke out slowly. And then, there's the look — his eyes, his mouth — and so much more behind his eyes and mouth. Satisfaction, relief, pride, humor. But even way more than these. Love and hope too, because this is his last gig, and there's a woman waiting for him who's the end of his dreams. I don't know, maybe a whole lot more we'll never know about. But I could watch it all day, like I would the Mona Lisa.

Or, we're with The Fellowship of the Ring, *on the bridge of Khazad Dum. Gandalf has followed the Balrog into shadow. He's gone, the leader of the fellowship, the one everyone looked to for wisdom, for power. And Aragorn, he calls himself Strider when he can't accept his true destiny, sends the fellowship out into the sunlight. But he lingers for a moment, dodges orc arrows shot at him from out of the dark above.*

And there it is, so poignant it still makes me cry: the look. Mourning for the loss of his dear friend and guide, a fleeting wisp of despair, perhaps, and doubt. And then the steel of resolve hardens him. Right before our eyes he takes up the mantle of leadership of the fellowship, not because he's a power freak, but the opposite. Because he accepts his destiny, even though it makes him more alone than ever. He takes a big breath, and then he hurries after the fellowship to guide them the rest of the way.

There's a look that's imprinted indelibly on my consciousness, from one of the War Zone's most epic films, that's worth seeing again and again. It's the opening scene sequence of *Gladiator*, the movie we've already discussed in another context. I know, when it come to Ridley Scott, I'm hardly impartial. But, for me, he's the best. I can always, always recognize a Ridley Scott film. He just does that thing. You know, that, that, oh well, another time perhaps we'll talk about how to recognize that special thing directors do, where it'll take you about half a minute, then you'll know whose movie you're in.

The first shot is a hand. We'll figure it out later that it's the main character's, Maximus, played by Russell Crowe, one of the great actors working today. The hand waves through a field of wheat to the sound of a child's laughter. And right away we can figure this is the flick's good womb. This is home. The Safe Zone. This is peace.

Quickly, the scene shifts, and we have a close-up of Maximus. And there it is, another look, one I'll never tire of seeing. Haunted, tired, fierce, resolved, loyal, and so much more. And what we see is that the hand through the wheat was his, and this is his memory. On the edge of another fierce battle, one of many he's fought for his emperor, and for Rome. And we know where his heart is — in the field of wheat, which has to be his home, and with a child, and a woman.

Suddenly, against the bleak, muddy background of the winter battlefield, the camera lingers on a multi-colored bird on a dead branch. And then on Maximus' face. The warrior softens, melts. His eyes sparkle. A smile of wonder and sweetness plays across his lips. The bird takes flight, and for a second, Maximus' eyes follow it with longing way into the sky. You just know it reminds him of where the wheat field is.

Then he looks back to earth. And to see that smile of sweet wonder dissolve into the face of a deadly killer general, a battle lord, is an amazing thing to behold. Here is a man, both actor and character, capable of an amazingly wide bandwidth of emotions and passions. But right now he's going to battle, and we pity those who stand in his way. So, that's the look. But it's just a preamble to the scene we want to talk about from *Gladiator*: the battle between the Romans and the Gauls.

Now, anybody can film a battle. But what elevates one above another, separates it from all the rest? What we're looking for is a scene that touches us, not just in the gut, not just where the adrenalin pumps. There's got to be something more, some other level of power that sublimates the struggle and gives it a cosmic significance.

Two things can do that. First is the content of the scene itself, the story, what the antagonists are actually fighting for. Like an *Alamo*, a pass at Thermopylae, as in *300*, a last stand. Or for home and hearth, that kind of thing. The second is that the battle can be shot in such a way that the death/rebirth struggle seems to be played out right there on the battlefield. Everything somehow assumes epic proportions. And we the viewers get a taste of war as an archetype, almost as a struggle between the gods themselves.

Some filmmakers can pull this off. Sam Peckinpah used to do it in his westerns. Mel Gibson did it in *Braveheart*. Spielberg, too, in *Saving Private Ryan*. And Malick definitely achieved it in *The Thin Red Line*. It's there in David Lean's *Lawrence of Arabia*, Anthony Minghella's *Cold Mountain*, Akira Kurosawa's *Ran*, and even Oliver Stone's *Platoon*. Certainly also, it's present in its most powerful form in Peter Jackson's trilogy *The Lord of the Rings*. But it's here for real in *Gladiator*. (And, even though the studio butchered the first release of Scott's film *Kingdom of Heaven*, which, incidentally, has a director's cut that completely validates and redeems the movie, it's absolutely there too.)

Even the name *Gladiator* evokes that feeling. We're already elevated into some level of mythic combat. And Scott does not disappoint. Check out the two warrior tribes arrayed on the field against each other: one, the Romans, disciplined, battle-weary, ruthless, and money-backed — you can tell by all the hardware; the other wild, fierce, free, savage, and proud. The long shots, trenches, the vast field, the forest, the catapults. And then, the words by Maximus heard 'round the movie world': "At my signal, unleash hell." No way. How cool is that?

And this is exactly what happens on the screen. An engagement of total archetypal ferocity. Bloody, but way beyond blood. Horrible, but past that to some epic feeling of wonder at the nature of life and death itself. For our intents and purposes — for the journey we are taking now — it shows us deeply what it's like to engage in an epic struggle for our very existence. To fight for something we believe in. To power through all that stands in our way to achieve what we feel is the goal. The classic horizontal fight: a struggle with those outside ourselves for whatever it is we think we must have. The struggle for our place in the world.

This is the War Zone in its most primal, and yet most glorious. But, as we shall see, it's not all there is in this universe, either. Nor is a linear victory the outcome — not for us, not for Maximus — even though we may have fought for it and believed it to be so. So, onward to another corner of the battlefield, to different longings — darker, perhaps more sinister — but within us all, as this entire dimension surely is too.

Pulp "Friction"

On one level we can call the primal energy, generated in the War Zone, *anger*. On another, it's the biological fury of a fetus struggling to be born. On yet another, it's power. It could be personal power, could be divine power. Still again, it's passion, excitement, and creativity. And in the end, it's just plain energy. There are so many ways this energy manifests in our lives.

Sometimes, it's not just the subject matter that defines what level of the Hero's Journey a film is portraying. Every once in a while, it's the style that gives it away, the way the director does what he does. And this is definitely the case in Quentin Tarantino's film *Pulp Fiction*. There's a segment in this movie so filled with mania, that jittery, over-the-top nervousness that so characterizes energy run amok, that there's no way to watch it without getting triggered.

In our seminars, we'll be showing movie segments and be just getting through with showing examples of the depression and stuckness of the Trapped Zone in film. Then we'll play this segment, and the whole crowd just starts giggling and getting fidgety. The temperature in the room goes up a few degrees. And everybody's squirming and getting wired out. By the end, the room has exploded in unfocused, raw, free energy. It's a great time to go to lunch, take a break.

This is the vignette where Vincent, John Travolta, has had a night on the town with his gangster boss's girlfriend, Mia, played by Uma Thurman. Now Vincent's a junkie, and Mia accidentally OD's on his heroin, thinking it's cocaine. So Vincent is totally freaking and drives to his dealer's to see if he can get some help. He knows if Mia dies, he's going to be nothing but a "grease spot."

His dealer, Lance, Eric Stoltz, who's high as hell, too, gets Vincent's call. He runs to the window. And in a classic, 'you've-seen-it-hundred-times' kind of way, he throws up the shade. Or more specifically, like, on the night before Christmas, where the dude runs to the window and "throws up the sash." Vincent's car comes crashing onto his lawn. From here on in, it's high-speed, non-stop repartee, back and forth like Uzi fire, while the camera jerks and dances all over the place catching our heroes like wild-ass, manic-depressive, speed freak puppets hurling gutter language at each other until somebody drops.

But nobody drops. Except Mia, but she's already down, and foaming at the mouth. Eric's girlfriend, Rosanna Arquette, adds that perfect bitchy edge to the onslaught. And there's this nameless goth chick on the sofa, stoned, which, by her dead-ass blankness, only goes to show how crazy speeded up everything else is. The inside of the house flies apart like a Tom and Jerry cartoon on fast-forward. What's going on? They need to find "the little black book," "THE LITTLE BLACK MEDICAL BOOK!"

Mia needs a shot of adrenalin to start her heart. Everybody else in the scene is moving so fast, I guess the reason is so she can catch up with them. I've shown this scene in countries where English is not the native language, and usually there are subtitles, or we have a translator. But sometimes, you just have to go with it, and hope for the best. And even in those countries where just a few people know English, and those who do could in no way keep up with the speed of this rap, this scene evokes the same response. Everybody gets excited, seriously stoked. You swear you can feel the electricity in the room.

Vincent and Lance loom over Mia, who's fading fast. And as viewers, we are so amped and seduced by the onslaught of words that, when the time comes to plunge that gigantic needle straight into the bull's-eye painted on Mia's heart with a magic marker, we're all like, "Whoa, wait a minute. Oh hell." And after this we add, in our horror and squeamishness, "I can't look, but I have to."

And then, in the only slowed down moment in the entire scene, the needle's poised in mid-air, one drop of adrenalin glistening like a diamond from the steel spike, everybody in the audience — that's us — and somebody onscreen is going, "I wonder what's going to happen?" And somebody else says, "I was kind of wondering that myself." And then somebody else says, "That's not funny." And all of us out there in Movie Yoga land are agreeing all over the place, this ain't funny, except that it really is.

All we know is we don't need the adrenalin shot. Because we're already up. We're flying. 'Til the needle plunges. And then, as the camera holds its breath for a second, so do we. And when Mia suddenly sits up like this mad puppet from beyond and gasps, we do too. "If you're okay, say something," somebody asks. And even though it's Mia who finally says, "Something," it may as well have been us. Because by now, there is no more them and us. We're all one, the movie and the watchers, in some special zone that only initiates are allowed to enter, when the magic is just one hundred percent, crystal-sharp, perfectly, exactly right.

It's that energy that I mentioned, where life and death hang in the balance. Well, not exactly hanging in the balance. That would imply more of a Trapped Zone kind of feeling. Here, Mia's life is vibrating in the balance, so fast you got to rush to keep up. Everything turns out okay. She lives, Vincent gets her home, and Marcellus, his boss, is none the wiser. But all that's beside the point. That may be the Free Zone, another scene, perhaps, for another chapter, but believe me, the power of this sequence is the energy of the struggle. And when the rest comes, I'm just too wired to catch it.

The Dark Side of the Force

Have you ever had really twisted dreams — all blood, guts, and bizarre sex — that upset you, but maybe turned you on a little bit at the same time? Well, it's not the easiest thing to admit. Why is that, do you suppose? Shame, for one. More to the point, we don't want people to think we're perverts or serial killers, or just plain certifiable.

We'd be afraid psychiatrists would look at us through some kind of pop-cultural lens, as though we had serious Attention Deficit Disorder or narcissism issues, or whatever else the therapeutic flavor of the month is that tries to explain something way off the normal charts. Well, we may actually have some of those issues. But sometimes it seems that traditional diagnoses don't have the whole picture when it comes to understanding why we might experience these types of dreams or fantasies.

It's difficult to fully understand all of this kind of material if we just look through the usual limited lens, the one where human beings are only what happened to them from their births up to the present. But if you look through the lens of death and rebirth, or even just physical birth, and add to that the Jungian dimension of the archetypes, then unusual stuff like this makes more sense and doesn't feel nearly as crazy.

Take the demonic, for instance — that scary walk down the dark side. It's like "A Night on Bald Mountain," a scene from Walt Disney's masterpiece of animation, *Fantasia*, which we'll look at a little later. Yeah, like that, only a little more intense, or, actually, way more intense. Let's face it. These forces, and the feelings we have about them, are also part of the collective, the Big Picture of which we are a part. What's more, understanding them through the lens of birth dynamics clears up a lot of misconceptions we may have, as well as old negative charges that may be lingering in our consciousness. Then, instead of feeling crazy, we can feel like we're actually doing pretty well.

When people have a death/rebirth experience while doing any kind of deep inner work, experiences that feel 'demonic' happen right on the edge, the cusp, between the War Zone and the Free Zone. The War Zone, as we've been saying, is all about aggression, sexuality, and some form of the sacred.

Why Sacred? Let's say we're in the War Zone and approaching a metaphorical death at this cusp. This means we're getting near some kind of spiritual opening. Death/rebirth almost always involves feelings of a spiritual nature. Because when it happens, we're all just one more step closer to wholeness. Any time we give up a sense of separateness and feel more a part of humanity as a whole, getting yoked up, like we said in the beginning, we're more apt to interpret this, and feel this, in a sacred way.

But, if we haven't quite reached the spiritual dimension, that is, passed through all the intensity of the War Zone, then our spiritual impulse is going to get all mixed up with aggression and sexuality. So, we can get this unusual mix of feelings, dreams, and imagery from our unconscious. For example, we may get in touch with the demonic, which is a sort of profane spirituality.

"Ave Maria" was a treatment of the sacred from *Fantasia*, just as "A Night on Bald Mountain" was a treatment of the profane. What if the sacred and the profane are all entangled together? This can be unsettling. But it can also be attractive too, in a strange kind of way. And this is one of the reasons why so many people related to *Star Wars*. There was always the intriguing possibility of being seduced by the Dark Side. Its attraction includes power, sex, and spiritual urges coming at you all at once. Together they make quite a package.

Take, for example, vampires. What do you suppose the universal appeal is with them? It more than likely has a lot to do with sex, power, and a type of spiritual urge — surviving death and having other occult powers. This kind of material can be a turn on. As I said before, I'm a sucker, so to speak, for vampire movies. I like them all, even the terrible ones, except PG-13 ones, and, believe me, there are a lot of bad ones out there.

There's an incredible scene in Francis Ford Coppola's, *Bram Stoker's Dracula* that is a perfect snapshot of what we've been discussing here. Actually it feels like more than a snapshot. It's an experience. And it triggers us to see it. This is a damn good vampire flick. Not perfect, but really good. I'm talking about Bram Stoker's classic, original vampire tale, with Gary Oldman playing Dracula and Keanu Reeves as young Jonathan Harker.

This is Harker's first night in Count Dracula's castle. It's been an unsettling supper, to put it mildly. Now it's time for him to turn in. So Harker is lying in a big antique bed. And just before he nods off, we hear some eerie music and heavy female breathing. Next thing he knows, three vampire goddesses emerge out of his ornate quilt. And they're naked, except for wispy sheaths around their waists. They're like supermodel Medusas, snakes all writhing in their hair. But they're all extremely easy on the eyes.

So they begin to cast a spell on Harker. And it's not just your basic bite-in-the-neck kind of vampire thing. No way. These sirens are focused on other things they want to bite and suck blood from. The whole scene is very seductive. Dark, sensual, dangerous. It's hard not to watch. And it is impossible for Harker not to fall for these women. He is just about to cross the line into vampire-hood himself, when Count Dracula shows up, totally pissed off that his love slaves are getting some of Harker before he has a chance to. So, he scares them all half to death — except they're already dead. And they slink off like, well, gorgeous, half-naked vampires.

You know how I said everybody at the workshop watching the movie was manic and wild during the *Pulp Fiction* scene? Well, when we show this scene it's pretty quiet. Maybe there's a little squirming around — a couple of under-the-breath giggles. But that's just because, truth be told, this scene hits pretty close to home. By that I mean, it's seductive. Within the universe of archetypes, there are all kinds of experiences and feelings. And this one is there too, that power of the sensual, of sexual beauty and attraction, of death, danger, and love all mixed together into a strange kind of upside-down spirituality.

This upside-down spirituality is archetypal. That is, it's common to all of us. Maybe not actively, out in the world, but it's there in our psyches, just as straightforward spirituality is. Sometimes, it comes up in dreams, and sometimes we may act it out unconsciously. But, as we said, experiencing it in a safe setting, owning it, and letting it go, like when we were talking about violence, are the surest ways not to act it out in the world. Well, maybe we can go act it out just a little bit? I mean, what would you do if you were all freed up, no commitments, and some gorgeous, undead hottie of the right gender for you came to your door and asked you if you wanted to go out and play? Never mind. Don't answer that.

In the Dark Queen's Chamber

You may have read the side bar a little earlier called *Looks*. If you didn't yet, I said there we had one more serious War Zone look coming up. Well here she is: It's Ripley, Sigourney Weaver, in the sequel to *Alien* — James Cameron's *Aliens*. Actually Ripley's nothing but intense looks, from *Alien* to *Alien Resurrection*, and everything in between (*Aliens* and *Alien 3*). She has to be one of the most intense heroines, or heroes for that matter, in all action adventure films.

Sequels

Weaver was able to work with some special directors: Ridley Scott, James Cameron, David Fincher (although they short-changed Fincher's budget, which really hampered this amazing director), and also Jean-Pierre Jeunet. At some point during the quartet, some players in Hollywood blew off the famous artist, H. R. Giger, who received the Oscar for his creature in Alien, *but who didn't receive the recognition he should have for the rest of the films.*

Many times, after you have a successful first movie, if it's in any way possible, they'll do a sequel. And too often, it's not as good as the first one. The movie just lies there up on the screen, and it's hard to get a pulse, either from me or the movie. But sometimes they surprise us. For example, the Godfather *stayed with Coppola, and Christopher Nolan did* Batman Begins *and* Dark Knight — *a brilliant film, not just a super-hero flick. It was also way smart to stay with Sam Raimi for the* Spiderman *series.*

Hanging with George Miller all through the Road Warrior *trilogy totally worked. And letting Guillermo del Toro do the second* Blade *movie was like icing on the cake, because the first one was pretty good, too. Del Toro's two* Hellboys *were magical as well, and he just let his mythic sensibilities go wild in the second one. Can't wait for* The Hobbit *and the transition film to the* Trilogy. *He's about the only one who could follow Peter Jackson's act. And then going with Alfonso Cuaron, who did the amazing coming-of-age story set in Mexico,* Y Tu Mama Tambien, *to direct one of the* Harry Potter *movies. This is just a small sample of how a sequel can be as good or better than the first movie.*

In the first Alien, *Ridley Scott created the blueprint for an entire new genre of horror. How many directors can you say created the blueprint for a whole new genre, not just once, but twice, like Ridley did? With* Alien, *but also with* Bladerunner *for sci-fi. And after* Alien, *then James Cameron added his epic, smart, lightning-edited action. David Fincher did an interesting, existential take on the third one; it was dark and moody. Although I got mad when he killed off Kyle and Newt, the little girl. They were two of the big reasons why* Aliens *worked, and I thought they deserved a chance to live and struggle though another saga. They were heroes. I still grieve those two. And Jean-Pierre Jeunet, who did* City of Lost Children, *brought that same dark sensibility he used there to the last* Alien *movie,* Alien Resurrection.

The War Zone

There's a scene sequence, nine minutes and thirty-nine seconds into Chapter 30 of the *Aliens* DVD, that's like one-stop shopping for the War Zone, as well as for a glimpse into the Free Zone. Ripley has just rescued the little girl, Newt, from one of the alien cocoons. And she's fighting her way out of this alien-infested complex, when, all of a sudden, they stumble into hell.

When Ripley looks up, she doesn't get it yet. Everything's been happening triple time, so much shooting and running and rescuing going on. All of a sudden, it's dead quiet, except for some breathing, which is more like a deep hiss. And this awful sucking, gooey, squishy sound. She holds Newt in one arm and her high-powered space gun in the other, and looks around real slow.

For me, this is one of the unforgettable set-ups in sci-fi adventure. They've just landed in the egg chamber of the alien queen, the baddest alien of them all. The camera pulls back. Ripley and Newt shimmer in the hot air. They're standing in the middle of a field of egg pods, each one home to a nasty little baby squid-type alien thing that'll latch onto your face, run a tube down your throat, and deposit a little alien critter inside you who'll then eat his way out of your chest when he's damn good and ready.

But that's not all. All these full-grown alien drones of the queen are hanging out in the shadows, just waiting to get to Ripley and Newt. But that still isn't all. Because there's the queen, this huge black, Hindu goddess Kali-looking type creature from some nightmare myth. She's on what may as well be a throne, slowly depositing alien eggs through this grotesque wormy tube thing into pods all over the chamber floor. Ripley has a look on her face, like "Oh, s—t."

The queen breathes her serious alien hiss at the intrusion, and her mouth extends obscenely in her razor-toothed set of phallic jaws, drooling acid. It's a standoff between two of the greatest arch-enemy women in action film. Ripley edges back toward the door. She stops. Thinks for a beat. And then, here comes that look. If it's possible, she gets a shade grimmer. She pauses. Then, in a "what the hell, why not" kind of little shrug, she cocks her head just a bit, does a half smile, makes in that instant some kind of inner decision, and proceeds to rain down termination on a whole lot of aliens.

First she lights the place up with her flamethrower. And when that's gone, she machine-guns any alien drones stupid enough to get in her way. And when that one's empty, she launches grenades into the eggs and the queen's hatching tube. And when she's out of that, she runs like hell, packing Newt the whole time. But there are two things she still has to worry about: one, the queen's pissed and coming for her. And two, she's got two minutes to reach maximum safe distance before the whole planet gets nuked from orbit.

They make it to an elevator and head for the surface. The factory complex is in flames. Huge fiery explosions are bringing pieces of it down all around them. The queen is on the next elevator up, right behind them. Ripley and Newt reach the surface and stumble out to the landing platform where Bishop, the robot, is supposed to be waiting with a landing craft to rescue them and get the hell out of there. But, no Bishop.

They stagger there in the wind and fire, while gantries and towers collapse in flames around them. The elevator opens, and here comes the queen. Ripley puts her hands over Newt's face. "Close your eyes, baby," she says to the one she promised to protect, and has managed to save through everything but this. And just before the dark queen rips them to shreds, Bishop swoops in with the ship. They scramble aboard and haul ass. The planetary computer counts it down, "Ten, nine. . " You've heard that one plenty.

And when they're barely at minimum safe distance, the planet blows, with what the Hindu epic, the *Baghavad Gita*, calls the "light of ten thousand suns." The rescue craft flies away into the star-filled sky. "We made it, baby," Ripley says. "I knew you'd come," Newt replies. They came through. And they're safe. For now.

This is what you call putting your heroine up a tree and throwing rocks at her and then tossing some serious mega-boulders. Let's look at all the death/rebirth elements here: First, we have this spot-on symbolism of the mother trying to protect her child. Or the child-in-jeopardy kind of thing you get during the birth of a baby sometimes. Next, there's major fire, which we always see in apocalyptic destruction: Ripley's flamethrower, the planet about to blow up, and so on. Remember how we said the final stage of the death could be like an Armageddon or an apocalypse? A planet blowing up qualifies as apocalypse.

Here's something interesting about fire in this context: It has two elements. One, it totally destroys, and so represents the annihilation of the false self: all that's old. But fire is also a cleansing: maybe a burning off of all that's poison, or impure, like cauterizing. We might be able to use a made-up word for it, such as *pyrocatharsis*. Cary and I took lessons from our birth coach for the home birth of Bryn. The coach said that when the baby's head is coming out, this is called the ring of fire. This sounds like a synchronistic connection between psycho-spiritual death/rebirth and actual biological birth.

So, if we combine all this fire, and the impending death of Ripley and the child, it's totally symbolic of the stage where the false self is being prepared for extinction. She did everything she could to live, but it wasn't enough. The ship wasn't there to carry her away. In the end, she surrendered. She had to. It was the end. "Close your eyes, baby." That's what she said when she knew it was all over. And then, out of nowhere comes the miraculous rescue, which symbolizes the beginning of the rebirth. When you feel as though you've died, or are about to die, then rebirth definitely feels miraculous.

There's a famous rebirth myth about a bird, the phoenix, which builds a nest and lays an egg. A fire burns the egg and the nest and then the new bird rises out of the conflagration of itself. Ripley's and Newt's rescue by Bishop is the phoenix rising from the ashes of the death of the old. When the planet blows behind her, it's the fiery destruction of the false self. And then the peaceful aftermath, the ship sailing into a field of tranquil stars, represents the new birth: light at the end of the tunnel, calm after the storm, the pot of gold at the end of the rainbow, the Free Zone.

No wonder so many action movies go Boom! at the end, even if they don't often follow through with a rebirth worthy of the Boom. But the psyche knows how rebirth feels. We might not realize it out here in our everyday lives, but we do when we see it in a powerful film. And when it actually happens to us.

There's one more major piece to this *Aliens* death/rebirth saga. And that's the presence of the dark alien queen, the dangerous mother. In the end, there was the mythic confrontation between Ripley and the queen, the light and the dark. We didn't cover before what I'm about to point out now, because I wanted to save it for this chapter. But frequently in the birth process — often in the Trapped Zone, but also in the War Zone — the death-dealing, swallowing, or engulfing aspect of the process itself can be symbolized by a monster figure, a spider, a giant snake, or even an alien queen. So Ripley has to face her alter-self: the dark mother. And her victory is like the victory of life over death.

Here's a side note about something I find kind of fascinating: I read a review of *Aliens* in an anthology by one of the best known and most well-loved and respected critics of our time. He gave it three and one half stars — just a half a star off his highest praise. He said he really dug the flick. But then he said something else totally revealing. He confessed that even though he felt *Aliens* was a well done movie on almost every level, when he left the theater he just plain felt bad. And he couldn't figure out exactly why.

Anybody reading this want to venture a guess why he didn't feel so good? You got it. He got activated by something. And trust me, there's plenty to get activated by in *Aliens*. Believe me, this is not a criticism of the critic. Of course he can get activated. We all do. He's got an Inner Healer and an Awareness Positioning System™ just like the rest of us. And his was just doing its job: bringing up something from his psyche, going, "Opportunity to heal! Opportunity to heal!"

Now, wouldn't it have been cool if he'd played Movie Yoga just then, took a look down the vertical, and seen what there was inside that was the source of the movie triggering him like it did? Critics already point the way for a lot of us, even if we ought to be relying a bit more on ourselves when it comes to opinions. But this Movie Yoga thing could turn them into a whole new species of "Way-showers," couldn't it?

With Extreme Prejudice

Believe it or not, there was life before *Bladerunner*. It was what I might call the *Apocalypse Now* cycle. And those were some kind of days. As *Bladerunner*'s Elden Tyrell, the replicant designer genius, told his 'prodigal son', the Nexus Six replicant, Roy Battie, "Revel in your time." And I too reveled in *Apocalypse Now*. Here's another "I'll never forget the opening shot" story.

This movie I'd read about. It got buzz for lots of reasons: it was directed by Francis Ford Coppola, the *Godfather* auteur; it had behind-the-scenes filming dramas; and it had a great story. I mean, one helluva story. Oh man, I was so hooked. The writer John Milius was trying to do the definitive Vietnam thing. So he took this incredible archetypal tale by Joseph Conrad, *The Heart of Darkness*, and re-tooled it for his war saga. The original short story was about a man who made a life-changing journey up river deep in Africa to meet this enigmatic character named Kurtz. That's one octave. A higher octave was that it was a journey of the soul back to its roots, or even back to some primal level of madness within the human psyche.

I'm seriously primed, not like at *Bladerunner* the first time, where the movie was way down my list of priorities for the moment. *Apocalypse Now* was priority one. So, off I go. The movie begins. The first thing I see is, well, not much — fog, I'm guessing — for just a few seconds I think it's fog. And then, out of the fog — no, wait, maybe it's smoke — the muffled *thwack* of helicopter blades. And there it is, and then it's gone quick, the chopper. But something else is emerging out of the smoke — music, a guitar — and once again, I'm gone, baby, gone.

"This is the end. Here it is old friend. This is the end, my only friend, the end" — *The End*, by the Doors — one of the great anthems of the Sixties counter-culture, and, you guessed it, one of the songs that shaped me and changed my life. And with those words, a napalm strike blossoms out of the rainforest, and now we got the lit-up stage for real.

It was as if some ancient Muse, the Show Mistress, the one that orchestrates the dramas of our lives, just pulled back the curtain, revealing me, with a front row seat — the only one there — my theater, my show — just like She sets the stage for each of us personally, perfectly, every moment of our lives, if we could but wake up and get the picture. Problem is, there's nobody sitting next to us in moments like these, to give us a wake-up elbow in the ribs. It's either our time, or it's not. And for me, this was one of those times.

A great stone god's face emerges out of the fire and the jungle, like a wil'o'th'wisp, and then it's gone. And the chopper blades become the thwack of a ceiling fan in a ratty hotel room. And through the blades the camera looks down, and we see a haunted man on a filthy bed with tombstones in his eyes. Then through the rest of the song we see into his personal hell, swilling down alcohol, silently screaming, squatting on the floor in a jungle ritual, shattering a mirror with his fist as he strikes out at his own horrific image, painting his face with his own blood.

And finally, as the music fades, he goes to the window, parts the blinds on a busy Southeast Asian street, and his voice-over says, "Saigon... shit." I'm there. You want to get there? Go get the movie. Don't read another word till you watch the movie, okay?

But, as usual, that's not the scene I want to talk about. This is just the set-up. Guess I needed to revel in my time. Just writing the words sends my soul. The Muse, our Inner Healer, is always, always there. She'll part the curtain on that show, any show — open up whatever world our longing cries for. Because She knows it's our longing that is her summons — the infinite zones, planets, universes that she can lay out before us, with one single purpose every time — our awakening, the quickening I talked about earlier, that changes us. As I said, it is available every minute, if only we could take the time to set the stage, ritualize it in some way.

Reminder: that's what we're doing with movies — ritualizing them: doing consciously, for the purpose of transformation, what we used to do unconsciously, just for fun. Do it like this, and then this ritual experience can show us how we can do it in any one of ten thousand other ways, too, all through our lives.

But back to *Apocalypse Now* and the scene I want to describe for the War Zone. Captain Willard is our hero's name. His mission: take a small crew and a boat way up river into Cambodia and terminate a rogue U.S. colonel named Kurtz, terminate with "extreme prejudice." So that's the thread that binds the whole tapestry. But what's really going on is like *The Heart of Darkness*: it's the journey of one man into the depths of his own soul to meet himself, to confront the darkness at the core of his being.

And why is it so dark there? Because we are evil at the core? No way. It's dark because we're just afraid to throw any kind of light on it. So, in the story, as the boat churns slowly back up river into the heart of darkness, the crew has a series of adventures that get more and more savage and primitive as they go. They gradually leave the outside trappings of so-called civilization — here represented by the high-tech wizardry of modern warfare. All of that gradually diminishes and becomes more primal the closer they get to Kurtz's compound and his rag-tag army of deserters and aboriginal tribesman deep in Cambodia.

The set-up for this scene is a crisis point they reach, beyond which, if they forge ahead, there's no turning back. One crew member has just been killed by a spear. They are in another world. Back in time, heading into the darkness, stripped of the thin veneer of civilization that covers what Carl Jung would call the vast realm of the archetypal unconscious. There are only three of them left: Willard and two subordinates, an easy-going New Orleans chef and a golden boy, a southern California surfer whacked out on LSD.

Willard finally tells them his mission, and that if they want to, they can turn back and he'll go on ahead by himself. But by now, the others are lost without him. The chef says, "We'll go, but on the boat. We'll go with you, but on the boat." Because the boat is the last vestige they have of the world they left behind, of safety, the only shred of modernity, so-called civilization that stands between them and the dark night. Beyond the boat, it's just the river and the jungle, and the river leads straight to Kurtz — the symbol of all the frightening unknown that haunts us from the depths of our beings when we are afraid to look.

So, remember the War Zone and where it leads: it culminates in the Free Zone — in rebirth. But you don't just waltz into rebirth, like the fantasy of an addict who wakes up in the morning, takes a shower, puts on clean clothes, and just decides he'll go to an AA meeting today and get clean. It doesn't work that way. There's a price to be paid. And that price is the death of something inside us that feels precious. That we'll cling to, even though it's like an anchor pulling us to a watery grave. We have to stand in the sometimes horrifically glaring light of our own souls, to allow ourselves to be confronted with the dark truths and murky motivations that often guide us. We are afraid to look at them, because we think that's all we are.

Of course it isn't all we are, but the kicker is that we are absolutely terrified that it is. And so we spend our lives running from some imagined evil or darkness that we think is special to us alone, but which, if we would stop and take a look, we'd find was archetypal, common to all people, and just a natural stage on the path of death and rebirth and our eventual transformation. Like the Moody Blues song says: "Ask the mirror on the wall. Who's that biggest fool of all? Don't you feel small. It happens to us all."

So this is the place we all get to in the War Zone, where we end up realizing what we are struggling with is not something outside us, but is in fact within. And it's also what is happening to Captain Willard. Confronting Colonel Kurtz is confronting himself. And here's how Coppola pulls off the journey into ourselves. The scene is only about two minutes long — but this kind of "two minutes" can be a lifetime, if, as I've said, we are awake to what it means.

The sound track is low, ominous, with a deep bass pulse that builds slowly, the camera like eyes in the bow of the boat winding up-stream through still, dark water. The jungle looms over the boat like hands. Long bony fingers of the forest weave a spell, threaten to take the boat and crush it as though it were an invading species, mad to attempt this assault on the heart of darkness.

Page by page, Willard tears out the dossier he has on Kurtz and tosses it in the boat's wake, the black water taking it down and out of sight. These pages are the last shreds of the modern mind sinking in the tarn — of no use here — in a world way more ancient and primeval than some petty semblance of modern psychological understanding. Willard, in the voice-over, says he can feel the current winding him upriver, plugging him straight into Colonel Kurtz — plugging him, really, straight into himself. And the closer he gets, the less he knows what he's going to do when he gets there.

The mist thickens; the green blackens with each passing click. The wreckage of a downed fighter-bomber smokes and burns from the top of a twisted tree hanging over the water, like some death lantern. They pass right under it. A forest of crosses looms on one shore, adorned with hundreds of skulls flickering in the light of altar fires. Ancient carven god heads loom out of the fog, then disappear, like phantoms. The boat itself is like some dark fetus on the birth canal of the river, inching its way toward some monumental apotheosis hidden by an impenetrable mist of fear — the future death, the rebirth we hope will come.

The mist clears. The music stops. A night bird calls. Kurtz's compound blooms like a poisonous orchid on the shore: it's a ruined temple, the unhallowed ground of some long-forgotten god. A slow drum beat, less than half a shaman's pulse, that's all: going *boom boom, boom boom*; waits a beat, then *boom boom, boom boom*, but soft, soft. That's all, that and the bubbling poles in the water; in the cove near the shore drift a flotilla of Neolithic canoes filled with silent, painted warriors.

Willard eases the boat toward the warriors from another time. It disappears among them. Colonel Kurtz waits for Willard in the bowels of a temple. And what happens next is another tale for another night. Welcome to the heart of darkness.

In many myths, as heroes face what Joseph Campbell calls the Supreme Ordeal, they have to die. There are countless ways this death happens. Sometimes they must kill some dragon, or an evil sorcerer. Often these deaths are the ritual deaths of some part of ourselves, something inauthentic, some old way of living in the world that we must outgrow.

No matter who or what dies, heroes get stripped of everything from the old outgrown life. This cleansing is required for the new thing to emerge. And always this death, in one way or the other, is required of us, in order for us to be reborn anew. So let's see what happens next: how our own river into the heart of darkness just may empty us, at its end, into an ocean of light no map has ever hinted was even there.

CHAPTER 11

DEATH

Gandalf: *End? No, the journey doesn't end here. There's another path; one that we all must take. The gray, rain-curtain of this world rolls back, and it will change to silver and glass, and then you see it.*

Pippin: *See what?*

Gandalf: *White shores; and beyond them, a far green country under a swift sunrise.*

~ Lord of the Rings: The Return of the King

Narrator: *On a long enough time line, the survival rate for everybody drops to zero.*

~ Fight Club

Leon, the replicant, to Deckard: *Wake up. Time to die.*

~ Bladerunner

Maximus, to his men, before battle: *If you find yourself alone, riding through green fields with the sun on your face, do not be troubled. For you are in Elysium, and you are already dead.*

~ Gladiator

Lord of Xibalba: *Death is the road to awe.*

~ The Fountain

Ada: *What a death. What a chance. What a surprise. My will has chosen life. Still it has had me spooked and many others besides!*

~ The Piano

So far on the journey, here's what's happened: We've left the Safe Zone, home, whether it's good or bad. We've gotten lost and stuck in the Trapped Zone, a timeless hell where there's no way out. And then in the War Zone we've found a light at the end of the tunnel, along with some power with which to reach it. After that, we've struggled toward the light, through all kinds of sometimes thrilling, sometimes sexy, but always violently intense episodes, until… until what?

Until we face what in the Hero's Journey is called the Supreme Ordeal. Now, you might think, at this point, we'd just kick some serious ass, win the battle, get the prize, marry the girl or guy, and then live happily ever after. But not quite yet. There's this little matter of death still out there in the dark, waiting for us.

Everything's probably started looking kind of rosy right about now. Smooth sailing, right on through to the other side. Except what we are horrified to discover, then, is that this is not just some linear struggle to an assured victory. Just whip some ass, then whip some more, and then, when we've whipped enough, it's all over. We win; get the limo ride through the confetti parade.

Now, of course this is the way a lot of stories end. But unless our heroes got put in some kind of serious jeopardy, like there was a real good chance they wouldn't get the parade, we really wouldn't bother going. Might as well stay home.

But what really happens in our lives, as well as in the good films, is that we're the ones who get the ass whuppin'. In fact, it gets so bad, that it can feel like the end of the world, the final Armageddon. In each genre, this beat down will have a particular look. In action adventures, it's pretty obvious: the heroine is in danger of losing her life. In comedies, it could be anything the heroine is in danger of losing: money, a job, prestige, you name it. And in romance, the crisis is whether the heroine wins true love or gets doomed to tragedy and sorrow. In all these situations, we want everything to work out, but for a while there, it feels impossible. Something important, huge, has to hang in the balance.

For us, it's as though we're a major player in the Apocalypse. Every world we've created for ourselves, all we know, or thought we knew, comes crashing down around us. We've fought as hard as we could, and now we're about to lose. It's all on fire, burning up around us. We've done our best, but it's not good enough. The struggle's too big. We can't win.

For the fetus in the physical birth struggle, this is the place where we can lose it, just give out, become exhausted. There may have been anesthesia. If that's the case, our struggles can feel like they're going to last forever, or we're not really going to get anywhere, even if we fight as hard as we can. Sometimes there's choking, or other physical complications; so death isn't just a metaphor anymore. It's a very real possibility. Here we are, so close to the light. Yet we are at the end of our rope. This nearness of the goal, coupled with the feeling that we'll never reach it, can feel so devastating, so hopeless, that we have no choice but to give up.

And when this fact begins to dawn, we still try to fight it with everything we've got left. But it won't make a difference, because, little by little, everything's slipping away. What felt like being on the verge of a great victory turns into our last stand, a bitter defeat. All our standards are in the dust. We're on the ground, on the edge of the precipice, looking death in the face. And it can feel at this point that we're actually about to die, not just metaphorically, but really, physically.

But even now, the expected physical death is signaling the end of something else: the death of our false self, the old us. The way we've always been in the world. And what our defeat on the battlefield — or wherever it is — means is that what we've been has not been sufficient to the task, whatever the task was. We have lost.

Ego Death

As I've said, metaphorical death, or the ego death as it's sometimes called, comes on the border between the War Zone and the Free Zone. By the way, have we looked at this word *ego* yet? In this day and age, we're all armchair Freuds. So we throw the word 'ego' around a lot. Most of the time we mean this puffed up pride part of ourselves, the part of us who thinks it's a big shot, or the coolest, or whatever. Now Freud actually had a real technical meaning for ego that's a good bit different. To put it simply, he said it's the part of our psyche that enables us to function in the everyday world.

If that's what it is, no wonder traditional therapists have a hard time when we talk about the ego death. Because that would mean we want the part that keeps us together to die. And if that happens, then we're all going to be serious basket cases and not be able to tie our own shoes or feed ourselves, or be functional at all in the world.

But there's another definition of ego that comes from the Jungian and spiritual traditions. In this one, the ego is a false self, a self contraction, that's been created by our patterns, our fears, and so on. And this is what we've been meaning the whole time when we talk about death and rebirth. Living in a false self keeps us constricted, feeling small and separated from ourselves, humanity, the planet, and the cosmos.

But, when this part of us dies, as we have been saying so often, then a new, more expanded or whole self can take its place. And the new self, by being connected, or yoked, as in yoga, enables us to live life in a much more fulfilling way. It seems important to make this distinction, just in case some of you are confused by this idea of the ego dying.

Test Screening: Death

Before we go through our rebirth, let's take a look at one terrific film that will set the stage for getting reborn. We've been covering some intense images and feelings lately. But every once in a while, it's a good idea to step back, take stock, so we can have a bit of perspective on this journey we've been test screening. It's easy to get lost in the details, and maybe not have the courage to see it all the way through.

Remember way, way back in *Finding Nemo*, the song of a gentle old manta ray as he took a bunch of little fishes for their first days of school? That sweet music, the peace, the feeling of being at home? And then, the edge of the deep, the boat — the Call to Adventure? How about our longing for some dream of perfection we may have known — *The Beach*. And the island in *The Thin Red Line* — the children and the mothers playing in the pool, the songs, the laughter, the games?

But then, the walls of the uterus contract. There's the first hint of danger. The crocodile slides into the swamp. The birth begins, and we feel it as the attack of a shark, like in *Jaws*. The wide-open peace of the island we saw begins to close in. We feel stuck, like in *Star Wars*. And we begin to lose the connectedness we feel, with the mother, with home. We feel trapped like Frodo in *The Return of the King*, encountering a great force of danger, like a giant spider pressing down on us, or ready to devour us. Or we're like an artificial child, looking to be real, as in *AI*. We're left alone, cast out, forced to take the journey by ourselves. And as we leave heaven, the road leads us to hell — down *Jacob's Ladder* to a world of aloneness, pain, horror, and misery, that feels like it's going to last forever. Or we find ourselves in a *Metropolis* universe of drudgery and meaninglessness. It really feels like there's no way out.

But suddenly there is a light at the end of the tunnel. And we feel a powerful *Pulp Fiction* type energy, where before we just felt like a blob. And we know now we can actually get moving, push through. It may take some anger and power, as in *Gladiator*. The path may take us through taboo feelings, *a la*

Bram Stoker's Dracula. Or farther up the river of madness, as in *Apocalypse Now*, confronting ourselves at the end. But we can also fight the good fight all the way and get closer and closer to the light until the battle may even feel like the end of the world, and we discover we may have to face our darkest side, as in *Aliens*.

Then, just when we think we're definitely going to win, we stand on the edge of losing everything. Here we are at death — what feels like the real end. Is this all there is? Or is there more? We know one thing for sure: it's been quite a ride. But what a shame if it were to be all over here. Let's see what comes next. After all, it's too late to turn back now.

Sky Burial

One of our greatest directors, Martin Scorsese, at one time studied to be a priest. Maybe that's one of the reasons the intense violence of so many of his films takes on that mythic dimension we've alluded to so much. He seems to understand the whole package, especially of the War Zone — violence, sexuality, and spirituality all together. One can experience these themes in his masterpiece *The Last Temptation of Christ*. And it's also woven all through his unforgettable story of the Dalai Lama, *Kundun*. It's from *Kundun* that we'll demonstrate death and that turning point where the sacred begins to enter the picture.

This is Chapter 9, fifty-seven minutes and forty-five seconds into the film. The segment is two minutes and thirty-two seconds long — two and one half minutes of devastating and haunting power. China is about to invade Tibet. The Dalai Lama's father has died, and monks are preparing for his funeral. The segment begins with monks wrapping the dead man's body in linen. This happens to the sound of bells and prayers, interspersed with camera shots of other monks who are doing the chanting.

For the rest of the sequence, we have two story-lines intercutting. The first is the funeral itself — what they call the sky burial. The second is a shot of the Dalai Lama walking in an open space with his advisors. There is a voice-over of the demands China is now placing on Tibet, which is being related to the Dalai Lama as he walks. What happens in the sky burial parallels what China is going to do to Tibet. Let's walk ourselves through it.

Imagine a high plateau among the clouds — vultures circling and crying overhead, getting ever closer. And a ring of vultures with wings spread, hopping among the bones of past dead. The vultures circle a group of monks and a body wrapped in linen. In the background, Philip Glass's mystic score and monks' chanting cast the scene with epic, sacred grandeur. The monks take long knives from beneath their robes and begin to sharpen them. They cut the linen from the body, while the vultures close in. Other monks circle those sharpening the knives, reciting ritual prayers for the passing of the dead man through the after-death planes and on to the clear light.

Next, the monks begin to cut the body into small pieces and mix the pieces with ritual substances. They then throw the pieces to the crowding vultures, who screech and fight over the flesh as they consume it. All this is happening amid the voice-over about how China is preparing to break up Tibet into little pieces.

It's basically the death of Tibet. So, here we have a ritual dismembering of a body and the dismembering of Tibet. We have death occurring in a spiritual context — prayers for the safe journey of the soul — and mourning for the death of a holy country amid hopes for its eventual rebirth and resurrection as a land of spiritual freedom.

Think back on the entire journey we have been through so far. Can you see how it has led up to this moment — to this death, the giving up of ourselves, the dismembering of those parts of ourselves that we call the ego, the false self? And how the vultures are not just carrion birds, but birds of ritual fire who consume the old self, allowing the new self to be set free? It may seem foreign to us in the West, accustomed as we are to our kinds of funerals and burials. But the spiritual power is unmistakable, here, high on a Tibetan plateau.

The combination of Tibetan culture, the music, the chanting, the ritual dismemberment of the body — all against the backdrop of the death of Tibet — creates an indelible imprint on our psyches in which the archetype of death and rebirth can begin to emerge into its fullness. I say "begin," because the full flowering is yet to occur. But we've come through something here. Its impact is palpable. So let's keep going, and see where this newfound feeling will take us.

THE FREE ZONE

CHAPTER 12

Rubin Hurricane Carter: *Hate put me in prison. Love's gonna bust me out.*

~ Hurricane

Izzy: *Every shadow, no matter how deep, is threatened by morning light.*

~ The Fountain

Colin: *Are you making this magic?*
Mary: *No, you are.*
Colin: *Just like in the story. It's like the whole universe is here in this garden.*

~ The Secret Garden

Pocahontas: *I will find joy in all that I see.*

~ The New World

We've lost. It's no joke. Everything — it's all over. Yet for a long time, still we struggle, because it is life and death. But in the end, there's only one thing we can do — surrender. Let go. And when that happens, everything shifts, one more time. If we're experiencing it biologically — if we're the fetus in the canal — this is when we're born. If we're experiencing it metaphorically or transformationally, this is when we die. And what comes next is our rebirth. At the end of our struggles, when everything has turned to darkness, we finally come into the light. We are reborn. We come through, just like the fetus. We are welcomed into a new world, as a new being. It's the end of struggle — the birth of freedom. We've arrived.

Once again, we're home. Except this time, it's not the innocence of our home in the Safe Zone before we took the journey. This time, we've fought for what's ours, failed, died, and come back new. And in the rebirth, because we surrendered, we won. It's not the linear victory we thought it would be, but new life through the great eternal cycle of death and rebirth that humans have gone through since time began. We've faced the Supreme Ordeal, come through it, been given the boon, the gift, whatever it is. And what's left is the journey back home. It's over. Everything is different and everything is the same.

Test Screening — The Free Zone

Prison Break

Have you ever noticed how, after the big Booms, the final shootouts, the High Noons, face-offs and all, that the "and they lived happily ever after" part often comes on-screen for just a little bit, and then it's over? I mean, the movie's over. We hardly ever get to linger on the reunited couple, or whomever or whatever was saved. Sure, we see them. We know it's happened. But the walk into the sunset is in quick-time. Ever wonder why they do it this way so much?

For one, that's the way they teach it in screenwriting school. Or at least all the books by the gurus I read. When it's over, it's over. Don't belabor the point. One of the few criticisms I saw of *The Return of the King* was that, after the climactic battles and outcome of the Ring story-line, the movie went on too long. You know, showing what the hobbits did later. I won't go into it here, because I've got one major tome I want to share about that consummate trilogy. But I will say that what Jackson did, besides just create a masterpiece and be true to the books at the same time, was give us plenty of time for rebirth, for the return Home after the Supreme Ordeal. He made the Freedom stage of the process just as important as the other three: Safe, Trapped, and War.

We have established that the Hollywood party line is, as my construction boss used to say, "Let's close this job on down." But that still doesn't really answer the question why. Do all the Hollywoods believe that we don't care about rebirth that much? Or is there some block in the collective psyche whereby we won't allow ourselves to fully embrace and experience what true completion feels like? Maybe we're a culture stuck on Trapped and Struggle, or War. Maybe Freedom needs to break free.

But in any event, this situation limits us a little in demonstrating the rebirth or Free Zone stage in film segments. We get a lot of "trapped" and "struggle," but just a little "safe" and "freedom." So what we have for the Free Zone is a whole lot of mini-segments where we get a glimpse of rebirth. And they usually come hand in hand with the end of the war phase. But let's look at a few, and see if we can get a little taste of what we've been leading up to for so long.

Remember all the examples we gave of feeling trapped and stuck? Like being in an insane asylum or in prison? Well, it stands to reason that busting out would be a major rebirth type experience. And one of the most powerful I've ever seen comes from *The Shawshank Redemption*, directed by Frank Darabont. So, we'll pick up the action in Chapter 32 of the DVD, one hour, fifty-eight minutes, and thirty-one seconds into the story. Again, it's short — just two minutes long — as I said, not much time for rebirth, but when you see it, you'll know deep down it's all we need.

The main character, Andy, played by Tim Robbins, has been in prison for years. After he's dug a tunnel into a utility shaft, now he just has to break a hole in a big sewer pipe and crawl on out of there. It's a big rainstorm outside, so when he slams a rock into the pipe to make a hole, he times it with the lightning and the thunder. When he busts it, a geyser showers him with filth. Then he climbs in. While he's crawling through the pipe, we get this dramatic voice-over by Morgan Freeman, who's been doing his voice-over thing the whole film.

Now Andy sloshes through the sewer pipe, and it's overwhelmingly gross. The voice-over goes something like: "Andy crawled through five hundred yards of shit-smelling foulness. I can't even imagine. Or maybe I just don't want to. That's the length of five football fields, just shy of half a mile." Meanwhile, we watch Andy slipping through — what? A birth canal! Full of messy, biological fluids. By the way, birth's just not neat. I was there at Bryn's birth. I've heard that angels are in the room, but we didn't see any angels. And even without angels, it was still one of the most powerful experiences of our lives, and very biological.

So, Andy is struggling through the pipe/canal. And the music by Thomas Newman is building toward a peak. Until finally Andy bursts out, or comes through, as the case may be. He falls into a creek, at night, in the middle of the thunderstorm. He gets to his feet in the water, as the music soars, and wades up stream, away from the filth. He takes off his shirt. By now the camera is above him like the rain itself, looking down on him. And Andy raises his arms to the camera, to the thunderstorm, to the heavens, and the lightning, with a look of ecstasy on his face, just as the score climaxes.

It's one of those moments that brings tears, where the heart can't help but leap. The filmmakers have succeeded. We've identified with Andy, hurt right along with him when the prison tortured him. When he breaks free, we break free with him. Just as his pain has helped us see the pain inside ourselves, his victory has awakened the memory, at least the archetype, of freedom that we all have access to, even if we've never truly known it in this life.

So, again, we have the two parallel dynamics. We have the metaphorical rebirth, which comes as his freedom from prison. But we also have the struggle through the biological birth canal, and then the coming through, into the arms of, what? Where's the midwife, the mother? In this case, it's the pure water of the creek after the horror of the sewer. It's the cleansing and purification of the rain from above that washes away painful memories as well as the literal shit he had to crawl through.

It brings to mind the classic song from The Who, as Roger Daltry sings, "Love, rain on me." Or it might be "reign o'er me." But it doesn't matter which, because this is rebirth. This is freedom. And like that tuning fork I've mentioned, it sets up a resonance in our hearts, an echo that makes us want to get up and run toward it with all our power. We might even begin to feel that we deserve it, just as we know Andy did.

The Movie Optimist

Sometimes my movie partners will roll their eyes at the movies I'll sneak off to see by myself. Like, those that we know are going to suck. So why will I go? I'm just a movie optimist. I believe I can always find something to move me, even if it's just a little thing that'll make it worthwhile. As I said before, maybe just a look. Or a ten-second piece of the soundtrack. One shot, some wide-angle vista, or a close-up. Two words out of somebody's mouth. I don't care. It's rare that there's absolutely nothing redeemable about my movie experiences — rare, but not impossible.

And when I get that little thing — well, it may be short in movie time, but it's not little to me — then what I paid for my ticket, my drink, chocolate, and popcorn is a serious bargain. Think about it. What would you pay for a feeling or a sensation that, after it's filed away as a memory, can emerge, anytime, anywhere, and fill you with inspiration, passion, and hope? Like I said, cheap therapy.

Dropping Armor

Like *The Shawshank Redemption*, the next Free Zone movie is way better than a flick with just one or two redeeming minutes. I'm talking about Roland Joffe's *The Mission*, a film with power, and with great performances by Robert De Niro and Jeremy Irons. Also it happens to have a soundtrack by Ennio Morricone that we use frequently in the work that we do, because it has such a perfect rebirth theme to it.

Irons plays a priest in South America who builds a mission way up a river in the mountain rainforest. And De Niro plays a soldier who kills his own brother, and who is destroyed by grief and guilt. De Niro's soldier is totally caught by these feelings in the Trapped Zone. But in movies, as you know, the way to convey feelings, is show, don't tell. So what Joffe does is create an unforgettable scene where De Niro's character is climbing the mountain with a suit of armor strapped to his back to the mission next to a raging river .

Obviously, this is his guilt and shame, but it's more than that, as we'll see in a minute. Now the priest is an uncompromising embodiment of the need for atonement and karmic payback. He knows the soldier has to free himself from this pain, so he doesn't give him any breaks. But the soldier's not looking for any either. He's so ruined by what he's done that, for all intents and purposes, he might as well be dead. He has no pity, or compassion, or forgiveness for himself.

After watching him drag the armor up the mountain, I identify so much with his pain that I almost wish I had the power to bestow compassion and forgiveness right onto the screen. Because I'd definitely bestow some at this point. But I bet I'm not the only one who can relate to this feeling of carrying guilt and shame. Isn't it possible that this is what we're supposed to be feeling here? Catharsis, identification with what the soldier's going through? If we do, then the film is succeeding.

They reach the edge of the valley where the mission is. And the soldier is covered in mud and sweat. As they say in recovery, he's hit bottom. He's a complete wreck of a man. This is what his shame and guilt have led him to. The Indians stand around him laughing, chattering at him in an unknown tongue. By now, the priest is filled with pity too. But the soldier won't let go. Somehow he's looking to the priest to absolve him — to let him know when he's been punished enough. But the priest won't take it away from him. He knows the soldier has to do it himself.

The Indians look at the priest, then back at the soldier. It's one of those magic convergences where everything, especially the fate of a human being, is up for grabs. An Indian takes a knife, leans over the soldier. He takes the soldier's head and pulls it up, exposing his neck. The knife is inches from his jugular. Then the Indian leans in and slashes — not the soldier's throat, but the rope that holds the bag of armor on his back. The armor falls away, drops off the cliff and into the raging river, where it disappears in the rapids, forever.

This was the turning point. The soldier's suffering ends, one way or the other. There are two ways death could have happened in that moment. One was physical — his throat cut, the soldier's suffering gone for good, with his body — over the cliff and into the torrent. Or, two, the knife cuts something else — as it finally did — the rope holding the armor. Again, it's the end of suffering, but in this case it's the ego death, not the physical death.

Watching De Niro here is like observing art. The sobs that he drags from himself, as the burden is lifted from his back — as it's lifted from his heart — are primal. He weeps with total abandon, with every fiber of his being. I don't know how he pulled it off. It's what we see in our work a lot, as participants free themselves from old pain, old selves. But they're not acting. It is absolutely authentic. This is rebirth.

The Indians, here totally innocent of this type of guilt and shame, laugh and dance around him as he frees himself. And the priest knows what's happening. He smiles and hugs the soldier, while the grief and the guilt turn to relief and freedom. This is what happens for us too — or can. We wear the worn-out self like a great sodden coat or a suit of armor. We've created it carefully for our whole lives, pattern by pattern, pain by pain. It is a real armor. It protects us from others and from the world.

There's an irony, too, because it protects us from the one thing we need, which is a connection with others. What's really getting protected is the false self, which fights viciously to stay alive. Until the crossroads, the magic moment, when some knife of truth and love cuts the burden from our backs. It happens when we've had enough.

In the world today, there are a couple of fascinating parallels with this story, where you have a crossroads experience with a choice between physical death and psycho-spiritual death/rebirth. The first has to do with addiction and recovery. I wrote a book about a new way to look at this issue. One of the main points was that addiction and recovery involved this very theme: death and rebirth.

Nearly all addicts arrive at a crossroads like the one in *The Mission*. There are two types of death they can go through. One, if they continue to use, they will die physically. Now, ironically, in order to find some kind of recovery, they also have to go through some other kind of death, the death of the defense system — a false self — that keeps the addiction active. That's just to get into recovery. But there's another whole level of death and rebirth too, and this has to do with on-going recovery: the Twelve Steps, or some kind of systematic daily psychological and spiritual practice.

But there's even a higher octave, another more all-encompassing level, to this addiction and death/rebirth issue. One way to describe the global crisis facing all of us, as a species, is that we seem to be addicted to power and greed. Here's an interesting question: using the map of the psyche as we've been doing, which of the four zones we've been looking at would you say Earth is most like right now — I mean primarily? Safe, Trapped, War, or Free?

No doubt it's, at least a little bit, each one. But I'd definitely go with the War Zone. It's like we're in the late stages of death and rebirth, where there is a titanic struggle going on. And the planetary collective ego is fighting as hard as it can to stay alive. But just like an individual addict, there seem to be two types of death we, that is, collective humanity, can go through. One, just like the addict, and also like the De Niro character in *The Mission,* we can face physical death. Only, at the global level this would be the destruction of the planet and the extinction of the human race. Sorry, but a lot of us don't see this as some kind of fantasy scenario. All we have to do is wake up just a little and take a good look around.

Or, instead of planetary extinction, we can go through some kind of deep psychological and spiritual change, which would be a whole lot of us going through individual death and rebirth, so that there's some kind of collective rebirth. This rebirth is also like what happened to the soldier in the film. And this rebirth would change, not just ourselves as individuals, but all of us. It would affect the way we relate to and deal with ecological, social, and economic realities, and all the great problems facing us today. And it would then be for the good of all, instead of for the selfish few.

Everything we've been doing relates to a larger kind of yoga, a spiritual practice for everyday life. Sure, it's based on movies, and it's about following our passion and having fun. But any spiritual practice worth its salt should be relevant and have meaning in some larger context than the one where we first used it. We should be able to see through a bigger lens, get a bigger picture, and have some unlooked for insights. That is, we should be able to make some connections between what we're doing here and the rest of life out there.

So I just wanted to touch on this parallel now, because *The Mission* made it so relevant here. Also, don't forget, we've finally entered the sacred dimension, at least a little. Because now we're dealing with the death of the old self. And as we said, when that small self dies and a more whole self takes its place, this is always a spiritual experience. But more on this later.

Off the Deep End

At the beginning of each episode of *Star Trek, the Next Generation*, Captain Picard, played by Patrick Stewart, would say, "Space, the final frontier." He's echoing the sentiment that says we humans have become accustomed to thinking we've finished exploring Earth. So, in order to satisfy that wanderlust, or the-grass-is-always-greener-over-there syndrome we have, we're going to have to get out there among the stars. But movies like *2001: A Space Odyssey* and 2007's masterpiece *Sunshine* add a new wrinkle to this axiom. Sure, space is a big mystery. But an even bigger one is the universe inside our psyches. So Kubrick and Boyle used space as a backdrop to take us on serious mind trips. Inner space: the final frontier. Has a ring to it, yeah?

James Cameron took us out there too, in *Aliens*, to show us something dark and exciting about human nature. And he's been real excited about Mars and any expeditions to the Red Planet that may be in the offing. But, you know what? His heart seems to be closer to home, here on Earth. Well, not exactly on Earth; more accurately, it's in the deep blue sea.

He took all those trips down to the Titanic when he was filming the mega-flick *Titanic*, and made plenty more trips for his Imax film, *Aliens of the Deep*. But one that gets overlooked a good bit, the movie that did for deep water what Kubrick and Boyle did for deep space, is *The Abyss*.

Here's the set-up: A marine lab runs into trouble, sinks, and traps its crew way down deep, right on the edge of a fathomless drop-off. Amid the obligatory running-out-of-air countdown, there's all manner of interpersonal action, intrigue, and villainy. On the edge of death, the crew sends a man, the always amazing Ed Harris, out of the lab, using some experimental technology whereby the oxygen in his system is replaced with water. Now he's like a human fish.

So he goes over the ledge into the abyss. And of course, there's a time limit — some technical thing that makes sense within the context of the film's dubious science. But who cares, because Cameron is a master of epic action, suspense, and intensity. But more than that, he's always created characters we care about and invited good actors to play them.

On top of this, he does a wondrous thing with Harris' descent. It goes on forever, down, down, and still more down. And this is where what has, up to this point, been a superior action/suspense movie takes on a totally different dimension. If this movie were a rocket ship heading up instead of down, out of earth's atmosphere, this would be the place where they fire the final booster. Because we're in orbit, with Harris. Except this orbit is a ride into darkness, mystery, and the unknown. It's more than just a physical descent. It's the epic journey of the soul deep into itself, to some never-before-felt core. This is the real final frontier.

Harris stops on a ledge deeper than humans have ever been — in a blue-black world, alone. His last few seconds tick away. He's in radio contact with the doomed station, miles above him, itself miles down. And on the other end of the line is the woman he loves. This is his death. He makes his peace. It matters, because Harris' character matters. We care because of the way he faced life, and the way he now faces death. He surrenders. There's no big fanfare. He's surrounded by silence — by a peace of the deep, the dark, the mystery. He says goodbye, and closes his eyes.

The camera's next point of view is far out in the abyss, where we can just barely make out a glimmering white spot that is Harris on the ledge. Then the camera pulls closer, and closer, until we are right up to his faceplate. And in the faceplate we see reflected a light. But not just any light. A light with form, with beauty and wonder, an alien creature. It's an angel of the deep, like some kind of mystic, marine butterfly — alien, otherworldly, yet sweetly human at the same time. This creature holds out its translucent hand, and the last thing Harris can manage is to reach out his hand too. And here in the abyss, in the middle of a popcorn flick, we have some kind of reverse ceiling of the Sistine Chapel, where God's and Adam's fingers touch, a cosmic connection being made between this world and a mystery far, far beyond.

The butterfly angel carries Harris through the vast world of the abyss, deeper and deeper, then out over the edge of another cliff onto blue-black plains of wavering light, a shimmering underwater city beyond all imagination. The score crescendos, and Harris' eyes are as filled with wonder as are ours, as the butterfly angel whisks him over the light world.

They descend again, and this time they are approaching a destination, some kind of tunnel ahead of them. And then into this tunnel, this birth canal, they fly, or swim, whatever; it feels like both. Faster and faster the angel carries him through the doorway between the world he's known and this other dimension. And finally, she/he drops him gently on a shimmering floor. He eases through a watery membrane into a cavern of light and silence. The only sound is his breath echoing through the crystal space.

He takes off his helmet. He chokes, gags up the water in his system. He takes the first big breath of his new life. And I swear, it's like a newborn taking that first breath. It's what we see a lot in the workshops we do, when people relive their birth. Now how did Cameron get this so right? I mean, did he know? Or was it just a good cosmic guess? I'm betting that he knew. In his movie *Terminator*, Sarah Connor, the woman the terminator is trying to kill, asks Kyle, who's trying to protect her, "What's it like coming through time?" And he replies, "I don't know. Birth, I guess. White light, pain." No kidding. That's tapped in.

Death and rebirth — what a journey. When the end is here, irrevocably, finally, when it's over, when we surrender, give up the fight, here is where the miraculous happens. Read through the mystic texts of the ages, and you will find tale after tale of this final ending, followed by the appearance of an angel. Or some being of light, the cosmic rescuer, who carries off the soul of the one who's dead to a new land and a new birth. And it's always into a realm of wonder that shatters the dead one's old ideas of reality.

It's so beautifully done here: the combination of psycho-spiritual death and rebirth, in parallel with images of physical birth. The coughing up of the amniotic fluid, the drawing of the first, big breath, the metamorphosis from our intra-uterine, aquatic existence into being creatures of air and breath. And Cameron pulls this off in the middle of an action flick, which makes it all the more full of wonder. We can make a calculated guess that there was going to be plenty of death. But who'd figure on the rebirth? He just plain took it to another level. In this kind of sudden magic, we the viewers are vulnerable, open to mystery and the possibility of great and sudden change. Now, this is using film as the Dream Factory was intended. This is truly working with a technology of the sacred.

Here at the End of All Things

Please, please, go see *The Lord of the Rings* trilogy now, if you haven't already — and even if you have. Because I promise, once you open to this Movie Yoga game, you will never, ever, see these movies, or any movies, in the same way again. I'm not saying you'll love the movies I love, but they'll be like new films altogether. Give it a try. But another reason I want you to see *Lord of the Rings* before you continue reading is because we're about to enter Middle Earth once more — this time, "here at the end of all things," where death can become rebirth and struggle can become freedom.

We last saw our hero Frodo strung up like a moth in the middle of Shelob's web, under the gargantuan weight of the mountains encircling Mordor. Need I say he got free, that Sam came back, that they found their way through Mordor and ten thousand orcs, to the slopes of Mount Doom? Or tell how Sam carried Frodo up the last of the slope, because the Ring had all but crushed him under its seductive power. How Gollum showed up again, of course he did, drawn to the Ring, his unholy bond with Frodo. How they fought desperately on the final slope and staggered into Mount Doom, the gates of fire, to the brink of the precipice over the lava river, the heart of hell. This was the only place in all Middle Earth where the Ring could be destroyed, if the bearer could but overcome the most compelling possibility in all the world: to be the possessor and wielder of perfect power, the Lord of all Middle Earth.

Remember when we were talking about Frodo's character arc? And I said we had one more "look" we'd explore later? Well, there are actually three that are like blueprints of this stage of transformation. The first is when he realizes he cannot go one step further: there on the knife-sharp, jagged crags of Mount Doom, right before Sam tells him, "I can't carry the Ring. But I can carry you." Even though, all over the world, great battles rage, fought by demi-god type heroes — elves, dwarfs, and human — the fate of Middle Earth has always been in the hands of a two-and-one-half-foot tall Hobbit, Frodo, who's made his way through trials beyond reckoning, the littlest, bravest wayfarer of them all.

From the Shire, his Safe Zone, through the Trapped Zone again and again into hell worlds that destroyed sorcerers of old, through War Zones and struggles that bested legendary heroes of mighty will and stature, finally, under the weight of the Ring, Frodo can go no farther. And all this is there, in Frodo's face. Thank you, Elijah Wood, for not acting, but actually summoning the archetype of Frodo from some hidden world and giving yourself over to him.

Pay attention to the sorrow, the exhaustion, the hopelessness, the defeat in that look, and then remember the smile we talked about, under the tree in the bright, care-free Shire, when he hears Gandalf's friendly song echoing through the gentle trees. A time has come for Frodo, like it will for all of us, if it hasn't already, when we have reached what feels like some kind of end, of finality. All the power we have summoned, from within ourselves, or with aid from somewhere else, to wage our battles in the War Zone can only take us so far, can only accomplish so much.

There may have been a time when we felt as though this power was a magic that would be unstoppable and would see us through any trial, all the way to an end that would be our triumph. But, here, on the slopes of our own Mount Doom, with the mystic gates almost in reach, we now have the sickening realization that we're going to fail. We've all been there, haven't we — this death of all our self-sufficiency — the prospect of some kind of annihilation of our cherished dreams, our very selves?

But Frodo is Everyperson. We are all Ringbearers. We use whatever power has been granted us in our lives: our minds, our voices, our looks, our physical strength, our cunning, whatever that thing is that makes us just a little bit unique. Whatever it is, we're going to run with it, because it's the thing that gives us juice, that exhilarates us, lets us feel special and different in a world filled with people like ourselves, looking for an edge. Our own Ring comes with all kinds of choices we can make — how to make that special power work — for ourselves, surely, which we have done most of the time.

But, if we're lucky, we might at some point awaken to the power of otherness, get yoked up, want to be there for others, perhaps use our powers toward some unselfish end. And how many times have we experienced these good intentions come to naught, because we couldn't foresee clearly all we needed to know, to see the big picture, to make the right decisions? We were blinded by something about ourselves we were unable to understand.

Or perhaps, in our innocent ignorance, we assumed we knew what was best for others, and ended up unwittingly controlling them, ostensibly for their good. But really we were driven by selfish motivations we weren't even aware of. How many times did our best intentions end up being no more than meddling in the lives of others, so that the end results left us, and the ones we tried to help, worse off than before?

This is what it means to be a Ringbearer. And as Aristotle would say (as he explores the downfall of another hero) our tragic flaw is actually believing we can be the one to use Power for good without hurting anyone else. And this confronts us, finally, with the ultimate question we'll have to ask ourselves at some point on our journey, "Can any of us truly wield Power, without hurting or even destroying ourselves and others?"

But I get so, so ahead of myself. I'm talking about a couple of books ahead, books that I want to write. Because how can we possibly explore, in two or three paragraphs, this dilemma of a lifetime, one that affects each and every one of us daily. It's an issue that affects us now, has always been with us, and will continue to have a huge impact on the world stage.

In a very real sense, one of the clearest, most potent ways to characterize what is wrong with our planet today would be to say we are all facing a problem of Power. How to work with it without being overcome by the negative forces inherent in those parts of ourselves that are selfish, greedy, and self-serving. And this is all the more relevant when we are trying to do something for the good of others. Because so often, when we help others, our true motive is to make ourselves look saintly. This is not just in our own eyes, but if we would really examine ourselves, what we are really doing is trying to get praise from others.

But I had to go there, even if it's just to tease us with questions of such enormous relevance. Because, truth be told, we must all face this issue on our journeys of transformation. And *The Lord of the Rings* just forges courageously ahead where even some great religions fear to tread. It puts the issue right in our faces. If we wield power, we will be corrupted. So what do we do? Well, let's see what happened to Frodo, and then try to figure something out from there. Besides, as I said, there are still two more "looks" we have to see.

Fast forward to the precipice over the river of fire — Frodo stands there alone, having run ahead of Sam and Gollum. All he has to do, now that he's reached the end of this incredible journey, against all odds, is toss the Ring into the lava from whence it came. Sam joins him after defeating Gollum. At least that's what he believes he's done.

He sees Frodo gazing out over the precipice, the lava light shimmering in his face. He begs Frodo to cast the Ring into the fire. Frodo turns to him — and here is that look — oh my god but we can hardly recognize him. All that we have grown to love, and I mean all, is gone. He is possessed by lust for Power; his soul is overshadowed, buried. He says, "The Ring is mine."

And I get chills even now as I write, and tears in my eyes. Because, I'm telling you, this is a look to end all looks. He has become the thing that is inside us all, which must be acknowledged at some point if we are to truly transform ourselves. It's that part of us that is totally out for Number One — and we all have it. It has finally emerged in Frodo and taken over.

And don't think it can happen only to Frodo. If we will be but just a little honest with ourselves, we'll recognize this seduction of power. We'll remember those times when we have been overshadowed by it, and allowed it to make decisions that caused pain to ourselves and all those around us. It is absolutely heart-breaking to see Frodo's fall, from innocence to struggle, defilement, and defeat. And thus, we get to experience our own potential downfall. But that makes it all the sweeter when death turns to rebirth.

Fast forward one more time, just a few moments: Frodo and Sam hurl themselves from the mouth of Mount Doom amid an earthquake of fire and collapsing mountain peaks. Yes, the Ring returned to the flames, Gollum with it. No, I'm not going to tell how this happened. Again, some things just have to be seen. But it happened, and now a purification is underway — what we might call a pyrocatharsis, a healing by fire. The old world is burning away. Frodo and Sam have succeeded, but that doesn't mean that they will get back to the Shire.

They climb a boulder protruding from the lava pouring from Mount Doom, an island in the stream of fiery death. They're dazed, in shock. Then the camera closes on Frodo's face, and we have the look: "It's gone," he says, in wonder that is way beyond relief. "I can see the Shire." His eyes are once more filled with light. But it's not the gentle light of innocence we saw in the Shire. It's a light of hard-won passage, of one who is coming through. This is a fire of rebirth beginning, but not yet fulfilled.

Have you ever been rescued, either physically or emotionally, from what felt like certain death, either physical or emotional? That moment is beyond words, a giddy burst of the power of life over annihilation, a sheer primal ecstasy at survival, as the life we have forsaken forever rushes in on us in an explosion of grace beyond the mind. Anyway, it's way more than this — words, once again, won't do it. But I tell you, it's in Frodo's face, that look — a moment of pure unfettered life celebration. And just plain, unmitigated relief.

But for Frodo and Sam, it's only a moment. An explosion rocks the boulder they're on. Lava comets rain down from the smoke-filled sky and burst all around them in gouts of red and white hot death. The world melts around them. It is only a matter of time. They gaze into each other's eyes and know it. They will not survive.

What follows is as poignant a scene as I have ever witnessed, as they share aloud what they will miss, all beautiful memories of the Shire. And though they weep while they say their final words, we can see surrender begin to settle sweetly over them, two dear friends who have gone beyond friendship to a love and a bond that no one would ever understand, even if they were to live to tell the tale.

They settle back against the stone as though it were something soft. They put their arms around each other, and one final time experience the lifetime of support — of having each other's back — they have given each other, over and over for a thousand adventures. This is their profoundly personal, shared experience: that against all odds they accomplished something that will reshape the future of the world, when not one other big-time hero could have.

And then come the words I was waiting for since the first time I saw the movie, and I still wait for every time I see it. And the reason I waited for them that first time was because when I first read the books, they were burned into my psyche like almost nothing has been since: Frodo says, "I'm glad to be with you, Samwise Gamgee. Here, at the end of all things."

And that's it. Kind of simple, really. Actually, not a big deal. And the reason it's not such a big thing is because, when surrender actually happens — and I don't mean some depressed resignation, or some egoed-out, fear-driven act of phony heroism — I'm talking about the real deal here — it really is simple.

That doesn't mean it's not profound, because it is. It doesn't mean it's not deep, because there's nothing deeper. It is a calm that goes beyond our understanding. Born of pain and sorrow beyond belief, sure. But to recognize, with all our being, what the Buddha called impermanence, not with the mind, but with the whole being — this is surrender, the acceptance of death, either physical or emotional, the death of our false self. That's the priceless gift of this scene.

And perhaps the story could have ended there, with the death, and it would have been altogether fulfilling. But it doesn't. There's more. How it could be any sweeter or more profound, I couldn't imagine. But it is. Fade to black: there are no words, either, for Howard Shore's soundtrack, here or in any other moment of the trilogy. But now, in this moment of their death, out of a bitter-sweet lament of angelic grief, and a glowing smoke-filled horizon, appears one, no, three winged shadows — no fell-beasts here, not this time. It's the lord of all eagles and two others. He carries Gandalf upon his back. They swoop in with a haunting cry and pick up Sam and Frodo in their talons, as gently as the sweetest mother ever held her child. And carry them to safety.

Unexpected, miraculous rescue — a profound theme in all the world's mystical traditions. Death and rebirth. Being carried from hell to heaven by an eagle, a solar bird — a common shamanic theme. But let's not get in our heads right now. Time enough later to do that thing. Let's stay with the experience of it. And maybe let ourselves sink into the possibility of that kind of miraculous rescue happening for us — or maybe it already has.

And if so, give yourself time to savor what that was like, or what it might be like. Miracle moments. Grace, like gentle lightning coming from where we don't have a clue — unlooked for, perhaps undeserved. Maybe that's why these moments are such gifts. As the *Lord of the Rings* trilogy is such a gift. Let's do ourselves a favor and savor the films. In this moment they're miracle enough.

A Fantasia on Memory Lane

A number of years ago, I had just finished reading a book, a modern retelling of the *Tibetan Book of the Dead*. Because of it, I had been thinking intensely about the death/rebirth experience. And here I am in this weird movie, *Fantasia*, Walt Disney's very early experiment in animation and music. I'm mesmerized by all these flowing colors and sounds, and all of a sudden there's an image of a coffin flowing down a stream. A coffin: something about, you guessed it, death, just what I was reading about. Have you ever had something like that happen? Some kind of coincidence that really jumps out at you, because it feels so meaningful?

Carl Jung called these coincidences "synchronicities." He believed they were signs, appearing in the outer world, but connected with some place deep inside us, that our lives had become greater than just a personal journey. Like maybe they had taken on epic proportions in some way that the whole world could relate to. He believed that synchronicities happened most frequently when we were going through something especially important or life-changing.

So, that was my first clue that something was up with this movie experience. From then on, each vignette in the movie felt absolutely personal to me, as important as life and death. It was as though I saw each one through new eyes — eyes that made the stories come alive for me. Even while I was seeing them, I couldn't tell whether what I saw was actually there, or whether I was getting a 'private screening', with insights written in just for me. Or if indeed my friends were even seeing the same movie I was.

By the time we came to the final two pieces, I felt entranced, transparent. It was like the movie and I had become one. I felt I'd thrown out all those filters I used in everyday life that kept me boxed in, thinking and feeling in the same old ways. I was identifying with the flow, the trip. Now, all this makes a great explanation, in hindsight. But I was definitely not analyzing myself while it was happening. I was just totally "in it" — feeling, experiencing, surrendering to the moments of image and music.

In my experience of *Fantasia* in those moments, everything seemed to be peaking in a perfect way. By that I mean I felt that there would be only one possible outcome, based on what had happened so far. Again I wondered, was this just about me, my perfect outcome? Or was it in the psyches of the filmmakers? The bigger question is, did they do it on purpose, or by accident? Don't all great films, from tragedy to comedy, build to some kind of crescendo? Is this because we intuitively recognize that we change and grow through upheaval?

Anyway, the conductor, who was the master of ceremonies giving little explanations and introductions to each piece, told us that these last two vignettes would be treatments of the profane and the sacred, as I alluded to in a previous chapter. The treatment on the profane was to the music of Mussorgsky, "A Night on Bald Mountain." The sacred would be set to the "Ave Maria," by Schubert.

I guess it's no surprise, based on what I told you about myself earlier, that I had always been fascinated by the dark side. I don't mean I would act it out. Well, not too much, anyway. I tortured only myself, and only psychologically and emotionally. But I mean that I thrilled to read it, to see it on the screen. I was always moved by the intense passion of violence, of sexuality, of the great dualities, like agony and ecstasy, war and peace, struggle and surrender. I loved Poe and Lovecraft, war movies, Westerns, and the great epics, like the *Iliad* and the *Odyssey*, all of which are filled with violence, sex, and huge passions. So I was ready for "A Night on Bald Mountain."

This was the point where I felt I knew the logical conclusion, the perfect peak, to a journey tailor-made for me. And I was right. It was wild. I was blown away. It was the greatest feeling that I'd ever had so far in my life. I knew it well. I rode that wave like it was my last. And in a profound way, it was. In the segment, a great demonic figure rises out of a mountain and conducts a wild orgiastic rite surrounded by his minions — imps, ghosts, witches, and creatures of the night. Somewhere toward the end of the demon orgy, a church bell tolls. Dawn is on the way. The creatures of the night cringe and slide off to graves and caves. And the lord of the demons looks up, raises his arms to heaven, almost like giving it the finger, and sinks back into Bald Mountain.

I was right there with him. I felt just like that. The demonic, orgiastic dancing was the peak of passion, the way I wanted to experience all of life. The bell tolling was the end of passion, of all the good times. It was like being a kid on Saturday night all over again, after watching some cool movie and having to go to bed, knowing on Sunday morning I was going to have to get up and go to church and feel bad for all my sins. As the Ave Maria started, I thought, with great disappointment and sarcasm, "Welcome to the sacred."

Then I thought, "My life is over." And I was right, but not in the way I figured at the time. "The thrill is gone," was all I could think. The scene was a procession of women bearing lanterns at twilight over an arching bridge, and through a forest glade. I was, like, so bored. And then, it got to me. I lost my breath. I put my hand on my heart and doubled over. A great wave of light and feeling poured over me, and I rocked back and forth in my seat. It came to me that I knew next to nothing about life, about anything. My previous cherished beliefs about what I felt was cool or worthless seemed ridiculous. I felt like I was becoming smaller and smaller, and I heard myself saying, like a mantra, "I am nothing. I am nothing."

The music soars, and the camera rises with the music, into light and a new dawn. And, then and there, I died. I don't mean physically, obviously. But what died was the human being I thought I was, what my place was in relation to other humans, to the earth, and to the cosmos. Right then, as it turned out, I began a relationship with some power larger than my "self". What began in that moment has always felt like a great mystery.

For many years, looking back on that procession of women in the scene, I could have sworn I remembered them carrying a coffin through that glade. Because wasn't that whole trip about me? I'll certainly never forget the coffin flowing away downstream near the beginning of the film. And to see the coffin again, at the end of the movie, in the forest, was perfect. Because this was my death. I was in the coffin. But, I'll tell you something interesting that makes sense after all we've explored about how these things happen. I recently saw the film again, and there is no coffin in the procession through the forest. At least not in the latest version I saw. But it sure felt like it was there that first time.

It was the end. But it was the beginning. I mean, I was new, and gloriously naive. I felt I had arrived. Well, I've died a hundred times since then, and I've had plenty of arrivals. And if I've learned anything, it's that death and rebirth are going to go on and on, at least for me.

When we came out of the theater, I was saying things to my friends — the ones who had watched the same movie, but definitely hadn't had the same reaction I did — things that not only had I never said before, but I didn't even know that I knew them. The kind of things you expect to hear either from someone who's spent years meditating in a cave, or else is locked up in a mental hospital. When they started looking at me funny, it was the first time I figured out I had to be careful with what I said. Joseph Campbell allegedly put it this way, when he was describing the difference between a psychotic and a mystic: "The mystic," he said, "knows who not to talk to."

The Return Home

There are classics just under the radar. Brilliant films that studios gave up on, sent straight to video, or banished to much smaller international markets. It's up to us to dive down deep, find them, and bring them to the light of day.

Here's one some close friends in Spain turned me on to. They kept calling it *Blueberry*, and I never could find it. It turns out they changed the name for the US DVD market. So, now it's called *Renegade* — it's got that popular culture ring to it. I mean, remember the market: dudes from eighteen to twenty-five. Which movie do you think they'd go see, given the choice: *Blueberry* or *Renegade*? A kind of fruit with loads of antioxidants or a tough dude? Enough said.

This is a Western, but not like any Western I've ever seen. Most Westerns involve some kind of action shoot-out. Here's a cardinal rule from screenwriting school: you're going to have a seriously dull flick, if you try to convey just what's happening between the ears. The action's got to be out here, external. Just as an example, I saw this anthropological flick, which was actual authentic footage of a shamanic ceremony in the Amazonian rainforest. The shamans had ingested a ritual substance and were sitting around a fire. This was late at night.

Sounds like a set-up for something powerful. But I'm talking boring. Just two men with their eyes closed sitting around a fire — for two full hours. They may have hummed a little or sung a couple of chants. There were frogs and a few other night sounds; that's when the tension was really high. Other than that — well, that was it. Now these guys were more than likely tripping the light fantastic; inside there, somewhere, it was probably Oscar time. But it damn sure wasn't on the screen. So, like I said, this is a perfect recipe for a quick death at the Cineplex.

But *Renegade* defied all the rules and got away with it — more than got away with it — created something radical and brand-new in the process. It's a Western, but it's a shamanic Western. By that I mean that the shootout, the climax, and all the other high points of the saga, took place in the inner worlds, while the protagonist and the antagonist were under the influence of ritual substances. But, unlike the anthropological movie I mentioned, the filmmakers created the inner landscape on screen. And it was a magnificent ride. Definitely some of the most powerful imagery and use of digital effects I've ever seen.

So, let's take up the action at the final shootout — gunfight at the OK Synapse Corral. We have the evil sorcerer and the fresh young novice, under the wise tutelage of the good elder shaman. It's perfect, epic story-telling: *Star Wars* in the Old West. The young apprentice has to face his Supreme Ordeal — confront the demons inside himself, go through his own death and rebirth — while at the same time fighting his arch nemesis, who, of course, is way more experienced than he is, so the odds don't look too good. And the wise shaman has to sit back and let the young one go through it, because you can't fight someone else's battles, can you?

Well, the confrontation is absolutely gorgeous and astounding to look at. The images are things I've never seen before on screen, and the music, a combination of instrumental variations and hauntingly beautiful native chants, just increases exponentially the power of what we see. In the end, our hero dies — not a physical death, of course. Instead, it's the one I've been talking about so much. And then he comes through and is reborn. And the evil shaman? Well, he dies too, but in his case it's the physical death.

This is the kind of victory they describe in recovery literature: surrendering to win, letting go in order to find ourselves. That's the paradox that goes so against the usual 'modern' mental framework, which tells us if we just fight hard enough we'll win out in the end. Well, we do win out in the end, but it's not because we just got a bigger hammer. It's because we threw the hammer down, and let whatever there was inside us, whatever we felt was after us, come on up, have its day, and then move on. That's a tough pill to swallow in Western culture. But we're probably going to find it's the only medicine we can take to save this planet of ours.

But back to *Renegade*. That was the death and rebirth. And if that were the end of the movie, it would still be one of the most innovative takes on deep spiritual experiences I've ever seen. But it doesn't stop there. There is some exquisite icing on this cake. And the icing turns out to be an amazingly authentic depiction of what happens frequently after the death and the rebirth have occurred.

We call this the Free Zone. And in *Renegade*, to see the hero find his freedom rings perfectly true. They have hit the note. He is free. Now, they're in a cave deep in some remote rugged mountains. So, after the hero comes back, there's a poignant and touching scene between him and the elder shaman — such love, such respect between them. Now it's brother to brother. The elder shaman welcomes the young one into the fellowship of those who, in the words of Jim Morrison, have broken "on through to the other side." "Watch your thoughts and feelings," is what the wise teacher tells the grateful dead, and rebirthed, young shaman. Sound vaguely familiar? Like what we've been saying all through *Movie Yoga*, right? Then the master tells his new brother to go on out, that she's waiting for him.

Now, who's this "she" waiting for him? The love of his life, of course, played by Juliet Lewis. So the shaman climbs out of the cave into the light of day. And we enter once again a place we've seen before and know so well: paradise, Eden, home, the Safe Zone. He sees his woman, naked in a pristine pool beneath a sparkling waterfall. Her sweet smile beckons him. He takes off his clothes and joins her in the pure water.

Next, we have a close-up of a majestic eagle — which is a classic symbol, in cultures everywhere and through all time, as a bird of rebirth. Remember when we talked about the descent into the Lower World, the dismemberment, and then the ascent into the Upper World? Well, the ascent frequently happens on the wings of a solar bird, or an eagle. So, in this scene, it's almost like the camera's point-of-view is through the eyes of the eagle, who swoops low over the green canyon, among majestic rock formations, and looks down on the lovers in the pool.

Then the camera leaves the eagle's eyes and shines up from within the depth of the pool, where the young shaman has dived. And he looks up into the open, welcoming body of his lover and ascends into her arms. There he merges with her, the archetypal joining of the Masculine and the Feminine, another symbol of rebirth, especially in the ancient alchemical tradition. But the perfect rebirth symbolism does not stop there. We are now given an articulate snapshot of one of the most important healing dynamics of the rebirth experience.

Remember we mentioned that there are some strong similarities between the first stage, the Safe Zone, and the fourth one, the Free Zone? One of the things we said was that they were both about a type of connectedness, about being home. Except in the Safe Zone it's the innocence of pre-experience — before we take the journey. And in the Free Zone it's the kind of safety and completeness we feel after we have had the experience of the journey.

One of the things we see all the time in our work is that, after seekers go through a rebirth, they often have a return to the innocence and safety of the womb experience. And it usually takes the form of a beautiful re-connection with the mother, either personal or archetypal — or the Feminine in general — again either personal or divine. The good news about this connection is that sometimes it's not just a reconnection. Because there may have been a toxic womb to start with, a situation which we've already covered previously. So, in this case then, the connection is a first-time thing. This can be incredibly healing, especially if previously there was a deep wound of aloneness, separation, or other trauma.

So this is what we have in *Renegade*. First, we have the hero's awakening to the beauty of nature, a classic rebirth scenario. Then we have his return to the womb, the amniotic universe, in this case, the beautiful pool beneath the waterfall. We also have his reconnection with the feminine, his lover. So it's definitely a personal healing. But that connection transcends just the personal and becomes his union with the archetypal Divine Mother and the universal Feminine dimension of existence.

Through this connection he finds a completion. Freedom and Safety have come together in a perfect example of how healing can happen. It's also an optimum strategy for living life here to the fullest. That is, to live in two dimensions at once, to be a complete and whole individual, yet at the same time to be a part of a larger wholeness, a wholeness where the individual exists, not as an isolated entity, but as soul among souls — free at last, yes, but no longer separate — our personal self joined to or yoked with, the Self, or wholeness.

In the final moments, the camera swoops above them, beyond the pool, and above the ring of mountains, the plains, into the clouds, and onward into the star-filled heaven. It's a perfect depiction of the unity between humanity and cosmos, between us and the Divine. And it's also a great place to end our test screenings.

Renegade demonstrates one of the great fruits of Movie Yoga. We can see it on the screen, but most importantly, we recognize that this is an experience that we can have as well.

And this is why I love Movie Yoga. I still can't get over what a deal this is. I get transformed while doing something I absolutely love. If that's cheating, so be it. I'll take my chances with my ticket, at the gates of Movie Heaven.

PART III

THE PLAYBOOK

CHAPTER 13

BEEN THERE, DONE THAT ... A LOT

Kicking Bird: *I was just thinking that of all the trails in this life there is one that matters most. It is the trail of a true human being.*

~ *Dances with Wolves*

Eric Liddel: *I believe God made me for a purpose, but he also made me fast. And when I run, I feel his pleasure.*

~ *Chariots of Fire*

Donkey: *We can stay up late, watch scary movies, and in the morning, I'm making waffles.*

~ *Shrek*

Buzz Lightyear: *To infinity and beyond!*

~ *Toy Story*

Okay, we've had what I hope is a bit of a magical adventure through some test screenings, and begun to get a feel for what to look for when we play Movie Yoga. In fact, we've actually reached a kind of natural conclusion to our Movie Yoga odyssey. Many of you are ready to play. If you sense you've got what you need to give this thing a go, then by all means, and with all my blessings, take the leap. You have only fantastic fun and life-changing inner rewards to look forward to.

But some of you may want a little more before you answer the Call to Adventure. If you're one of these, it's time now to fine-tune our insights and maybe get a playbook that'll make the game a piece of cake to play. Remember when we talked about one of humanity's most common mantras: "I can't believe this is happening to me again." If we've ever said this before — and you can bet we have — it tells us at least a couple of things about how we live our lives.

First, it's the refrain of what just might be the longest playing blues song we've ever sung: low-down self pity and consummate victim mentality. This would be the belief that says life is an outside job, that we don't have much say in shaping what happens to us.

Second, and this one is an interesting variation on the theme about us being playthings of the world, we could really be gearing up for one hellava self-recrimination session that would begin something like this: "I have to be amazingly stupid to keep making the same mistake over and over."

Now the interesting thing is, when we begin to do some work on ourselves — let's say, start playing by some of the Movie Yoga game guidelines we've been discussing — that lament comes out just a little differently. It's still a bit of a blues thing, but in another way it is poles apart from the one we just used. It goes something like this: "I can't believe I'm doing this one again." Do you see the difference?

The first one, "I can't believe this is happening to me again," is not taking responsibility for any part of what we're going through — blaming the world outside ourselves — and setting ourselves up permanently to be the world's pinball. But the second one, "I can't believe I'm doing this one again," is recognition of our co-creative responsibility for much of what we feel and experience in the world. More importantly, it reflects how we react to what happens, what we do, and the core belief that we are not just victims, but real players in our universe.

We must bring our Awareness Positioning System™ on line. The ability to be self-aware, to use our minds, and the power of our will, to focus inward — against the great seductive pull of our entire lifetime, which tells us that life only comes to us from the outside — is one of the greatest gifts of transformation. But in this game, this Movie Yoga universe, which I hope we're beginning to realize could be a blueprint for how to live every moment of our lives, it's not just about using our minds in a new and more self-empowering way. It's about letting our feelings guide us to change ourselves. It's about allowing them to be our allies, to show us something valuable about ourselves that we might otherwise miss.

When we play Movie Yoga for a while, we'll start to understand that those feelings we have, which seem to motivate us to do the things we do over and over, are not isolated incidences. They're not just random experiences that impact us in a scatter-shot kind of way. What they really begin to show us is the power of pattern in our lives. If we pay attention — use our awareness — we can begin to notice connections between events and emotions over a period of time. When this begins to happen, the game takes on a whole new dimension, and actually gets easier and more fun to play. We become like cosmic super-sleuths unraveling clues to the coolest mystery of them all: ourselves. Or we can even start to get the feeling that we're the scientists of our own experiments.

Imagine that these events, coupled with the feelings we have about them, which feel cut from the same mold as a lot of others, are like beads on a string. And the string is the pattern, the thread that brings them all together and shows us the power of the beads. Take any deep emotion: sadness, longing, anger, safety, fear, courage, love, ecstasy — on and on — and then imagine all the instances in your life where you have felt one of them. Trace the thread back through all those times as far as you can. What do we learn? That it's not just the feeling; it's the power of the pattern itself that motivates us, either in negative ways that challenge us, or in positive ways that enhance our overall life experience.

After we've traced the feelings via our APS down the vertical, and discovered the pattern, then we bring ourselves back to the present moment. The moment where we feel the feeling once again, like in a theater while we're playing Movie Yoga. And, depending on where we are on our own journey — how awake we are becoming — we make one or the other of these two statements: "I can't believe this is happening to me again." Or, "I can't believe I'm doing this one again." Our task at this point is to hear the call each of our Inner Healers are sending us. Like I said, it goes something like this, in a thousand different ways: "Opportunity to heal! Opportunity to heal!" If it's, "I can't believe I'm doing this one again," then that's a serious breakthrough. Take it to the bank.

If we are confused or overwhelmed by the power of the emotion, which can be pretty common, and lost in the situation that the emotion is coloring, this is where we can ask ourselves one or both of these questions: "Is this familiar?" "Have I ever felt this before?" When the answer is "yes," and I bet it will be, almost every time, we are immediately catapulted from victimhood to ownership, from reacting to acting. This simple re-focusing technique has huge implications for our well-being. It represents a crossroads. If we choose the road of these two questions, all of a sudden we are in new terrain whose principle characteristic is self-empowerment instead of dis-empowerment.

These two questions open the door to transformation. It's as if we are given a spotlight, or a telescope — really, it's the light of consciousness, or awareness itself — where we can look back through our lives and illuminate what before this has only been in shadow. We follow the thread back, as far as we are able. This is how we play Movie Yoga. We let ourselves feel, open to our gut feelings, our body memories. When we follow these things with this form of self-inquiry, we will be amazed just how clear and obvious the answers almost always are.

Most of the time, it will not be something we don't know — some big surprise. It will be as familiar to us as our hands. In a movie, it won't be coming from the screen. It will be coming from our lives. We can trust it. We can trust the Inner Healer — that power within us that helps us focus the light on what can heal us. Sure, some things about transformation are complicated. But a lot are simple, like making a habit out of asking ourselves these questions. This simple practice is a great place to start on the journey of self-exploration. And anybody can do it. Give it a try the next time you hear yourself saying, "I can't believe this is happening to me again."

The Twenty-Five Percent Solution

So let's imagine that we are changing our mantra about the pattern we fall into from instead of, "I can't believe this is happening to me again" to "I can't believe I'm doing this again,. When we do this, then three quarters of the game is won. The last quarter, the last twenty-five percent, is to have a strategy that will hopefully bring the pattern into our awareness and allow us to embrace it — that is, own it and accept it as being a part of us. And then find some kind of ritual to let it go. How do you do that? Any way that works for you.

Here are just a few possibilities: What I sometimes do, especially if I've already been practicing embracing it for a long time, is just throw it into this bright fire I see in my mind's eye. Like a big cleansing, a *pyrocatharsis*. Other people use prayer. Those in recovery frequently use the Sixth and Seventh Steps, becoming "entirely ready" for the pattern to be removed and then "humbly asking" their Higher Power to take it away.

There's a beautiful Buddhist meditation practice called Vipassana, or Mindfulness, that works well too. Here, you focus on the breath in sitting meditation. And when the feeling or pattern comes up, the strategy is to stay focused on the breath and let the issue go. Just stay as mindful and as unattached as you can. This is another practice where awareness itself is a healing power. The first step is to really be aware of it, the next is to name it, and the final one is, to let it go.

Another approach from the Buddhist tradition invites us to move toward and embrace those uncomfortable issues we become aware of, instead of shrinking from them, trying to avoid them, or shutting them out of our minds. We've grown up thinking that if we embrace them, it'll just make things worse. But the opposite is true. If we push them away, these issues will run after us, hound us. It's like they want to get our attention. And, it's important to keep coming back to this truth: it is attention — awareness, or consciousness — that is the healer.

These practices take a bit of fortitude. We have to kind of go for it, take a risk. Doing them over time actually brings a lot of inner peace, self-confidence, and healthy self-esteem. But it doesn't matter in what manner you let the stuff go. The important thing is to own the feeling or pattern first, take responsibility. By that I mean embrace it, instead of pushing it away. We put so much energy into not facing what's trying to get our attention. Then how we let it go is our own choice. Just as long as we do it, that's what counts.

Seeing Things You Wouldn't Believe

Okay, let's assume that by this time you've test-driven Movie Yoga. You went to the theater and tried a flick. And you had all kinds of good intentions. You even talked your partner into playing too. Then, wonder of wonders, you actually had some intense feelings come up. So far, so good. And when they did, you went, "Oh, all right, that's it — that's the game."

Like Samwise said the first time he hit an orc up-side the head with his cooking pot, "I think I'm getting the hang of this thing." You say, "That's... mmm... no wait a minute, here comes some more movie." And then, "Oh, there's another feeling. Whoa, dude, I was just getting cranked up on that other one," and again, "Oh forget it, the movie's coming too fast. Feeling overload! Feeling overload! I thought I had it, but..."

So, now you're at the coffee shop after the flick and maybe a little bit wired. You had it, right there in the movie. But then, it got away from you, and you got frustrated. So you go, "I quit. This is bogus. I'm not going to play; it's too hard. But, you know what? Something did happen. Not quite sure what it was, but it wasn't nothing.

"There's like some kind of a rumbling in the jungle going on. I'm all hot and bothered, but I can't put my finger on it. Uh oh, wait a minute. I feel like maybe there's a — get outta here — a splinter in — I mean, no way. It's in my mind! Oh my god, it worked. I'm playing Movie Yoga! No, I'm not. I'm just making this up. I just had too many M&M's. I'm sugar-rushed out. I wish I never heard of this thing. Now I'm worse off than before. I'm, I'm..."

Hang on! What would you say if I told you that you were "in the pike, five by five," like the drop ship pilot in *Aliens* I mentioned way back said? That you actually nailed Movie Yoga — especially for a rookie. That this is exactly what's supposed to happen. You're getting rocked. What did you think was going down — you were just going to see a movie, feel something, then everything would be like all warm and fuzzy? Well, I wish that was all there was to it. I mean, maybe when we get our Movie Yoga chops down, it will be. But especially right out of the gate, it's bound to make us squirrely.

You remember when you started playing video games, how you had to get used to the controls? You don't play video games? Okay, you remember when you began anything, and you had to figure out how to get started? That's the way Movie Yoga is too. So what we're going to do is give you a little cheat sheet, a playbook kind of thing, just something you can doodle with while you're sipping your latte, about as heavy as Sudoku or a crossword puzzle. It'll help you get into the mindset that's got you frustrated maybe a little now, but can become second nature to you if you stay with it a while.

So, the way we're going to do it is to lay out some simple, easy-to-follow questions you can jot down some notes about. No big deal. Just a word or two about the feelings and sensations that came up for you in the movie. And just this little simple, sit-down process, can light a fire in you, break the log jam your emotions are in. Mobilize the force of the Inner Healer inside you, and then — well then, it's adventure time.

So here's a way to get started. After you play for a while, you probably won't need the cheat sheet. Like I said, this is just to get you on track. Now, take a breath, and go for it.

Your Friendly Grind House Emotional Survey

Now that you're out of the theater, the first thing is a basic check-in with yourself. Be sitting down, with your coffee, whatever. Take one or two deep breaths. That'll help you relax as well as focus. If you have a partner in crime, it might be fun to do this thing together.

Been There, Done That... A Lot

- Bring your Awareness Positioning Ssystem™ (APS) on line.

- Do a quick body scan — no worries. Relaxed? Tight? Tension anywhere specific? Headache? Warm and fuzzy? Horny? Here's a clue: Do you feel different than the way you felt when you sat down before the movie started?

- Jot down one word answers if it feels right, or share them with your running buddy. You don't have to do anything about how you're feeling except be aware. Just notice. Awareness is healing in and of itself.

- Now quick-scan your emotions. What's up right this minute? Keep it simple: Mad, sad, glad? Okay, you can go a little deeper if you want to: ecstatic, shamed, excited, afraid, grossed out, envious, peaceful, lonely? Once again, is it different from when you sat down before the movie started? Just be aware. Don't try to change anything, or make anything happen.

- So, what about if you're numb — can't feel anything? That's cool too. Just be aware of that — don't judge yourself if you can help it. Being numb is a totally legit reaction to what happens in movies. It can show you something important about yourself. It's a deep way to play the game.

- Okay, now you're on your way. Next, scan back over the movie. First, the big picture: What impression hits you most? Remember, this is not film appreciation class. Try to stay out of your head. Just feelings, as much as possible, like: I loved it. I hated it. It made me sick. It turned me on. It blew me away.

- Notice if you have a tendency to say, "The movie made me feel... (whatever it is)." If you find yourself doing this, keep referring to your APS to help you rephrase your feeling statement: "While seeing this movie, I felt... (whatever)," or, "After seeing it, I felt... (whatever)."

- Let's take it one step deeper: Do the same process for specific scenes, characters, a piece of the soundtrack, a line of dialogue — any part or parts of the movie that stand out. Here's how this will look: "When Eowyn killed the Lord of the Nazgul, I felt elated, vindicated, and thrilled." Or, "When I heard that Rocky theme song one more time, I felt like puking and wreaking some havoc, I was so disgusted and pissed off."

That's it. That's all there is to it. CONGRATULATIONS! Believe it or not, you just did it. You just played Movie Yoga. That wasn't too bad, was it? So, you're asking, "Is that all? What's the big deal?" Well, here's the big deal: like we've said over and over, the trip is to be aware. Feel good about yourself! You've ventured into territory ninety-nine percent of humanity is afraid to even think about.

Oh, but nothing happened? You aren't enlightened yet? Okay, take another couple of breaths. Here's what it's like, deep inside us: Our emotions are like this forty-feet-high log jam on a snowmelt-swollen Alaskan river. And we just tiptoed out there onto the middle of the jam and managed to pry loose one log. If we're lucky, we just got what loggers call the 'key log' moving. It's the one log that, when it's loose, will set into motion the gradual unjamming of all the logs and free up the river. Or maybe it's one of the other logs in the jam — they're all just as important. All we or the loggers have to do now is sit back, pay attention, and observe it happening.

So, how do we do that? Well, go on and do your life. Better yet, rent another flick. Play it again. Notice. Notice what? Everything you can — your everyday reactions, whatever. Start keeping some notes — draw a picture. Little by little that log jam is breaking up. Oh, feeling courageous? You want more? Good on ya'. Here's another level of Movie Yoga.

Your Slightly More Intense Grind House Emotional Survey

You can use the same flick you just did, or a new one. If it's a different one, follow the same guidelines you did the first time. Only this time, we're going to add a few more steps. Ready?

❧ After you've discovered a feeling, ask yourself one or both of the following questions: Is this feeling familiar? Have I ever felt it before?

❧ If the answer is yes, stop for a second. Take a couple of deep breaths. Bring your Awareness Positioning System™ (APS) online. Now, try to remember where or when you last felt it. If you can do this, jot it down — just a couple of words — scribble a picture, whatever. This'll help anchor it, bring it to life. Or tell your movie partner in crime. Now stop... let yourself feel. Don't try to do anything about it. Just feel.

❧ Okay, now use the last time you felt this thing as a jumping off place, and try to remember the last time you felt it before that. Got it? Put it down, tell your running buddy, file it.

❧ Now, do it again — the time even before that last time. Take another breath. Only now, imagine when you take that breath, you're breathing in all the times you felt that thing. The Whole Pattern. Go for it, all the way back. Let it be like a veil parting, and all of a sudden you get this telescopic vista. A powerful spotlight. Ride that light all the way back. Let yourself see it, if you can, those old times. Let yourself feel.

❧ If you find yourself wanting to run, just notice that. Keep paying attention, as best you can. Do your best to embrace the pattern. Breathe it in. Put it on paper — just a note. Share it with your friend, whatever.

❧ Now, go up to the paragraph above the previous one and try one that feels right. Envision a fire in your mind. Throw the pattern in. But don't throw it in until you embrace it. You've got to embrace it before you let it go. If you're in the Program, work a Sixth and Seventh Step on it. If you have a Higher Power or a source of inspiration, say a prayer. If you have a meditation practice, do it.

❧ It you don't regularly do anything, do something! Even if you think it's wrong, or crazy. Make something up. Be original. Hell, you are original. Be aware. Pay attention as best you can. That's all that's required. A mentor told me one time: A frog sitting on a lily pad makes a decision to jump, he's still sitting there. He's still got to jump. So, jump!

All right. Take one more good breath. That's enough for now. Good work, Frodo, or Lyra, from *The Golden Compass*, you adventurer, you. Feel good about what you just did. You deserve it. One final word: You can't do this thing wrong. Even if you became freaked out at what you saw, just pay attention to that. The ground moving under you a little? More power to you. You know what? You can handle it. Stay with what you got — your notes, what you just saw and felt. Don't isolate from other people, if you can help it. Get your running buddy, and see the movie again, or a different one. Remember, yoga means to connect up.

You're like Neo in *The Matrix*, just after Morpheus and Trinity and the crew of the Nebuchadnezzar woke him up, rescued him from his womb pod, and he's opening his eyes on deck for the first time, and Morpheus says, "Welcome to the desert of the Real." And even if the Real is out of your comfort zone, you can count on at least one way cool thing: you're more awake than you've ever been. Even if it's on the edge, you're alive in a way you've never felt. It's a new dawn. It's a new day. Would you ever really want to go back? Could you?

When It's Too Much Like Work

One more thing: The questions we just laid out? They're merely guidelines. It's for if you have no clue where to start with Movie Yoga. It's about as simple as I could make it, but for a lot of us it may still seem like work. Many of you won't even need it — especially if you're already accustomed to doing some introspection. Like, you've done therapy, or meditation, or whatever, before. Or, you have super easy access to your APS. If that's the case, skip this stuff. You ought to be able to just play as you go.

By that, I mean, while you're in the theater, in the moment, the whole process that just got outlined that you'd do in the coffee shop after the flick, you can do right then, in the middle of the movie, whenever a feeling strikes you. You don't even have to bring your APS on-line, because it already is. Feel the hit from the movie, the trigger coming at you on the horizontal arm of the plus sign. Then just take it, cruise down the vertical arm, and kaching! — it'll be like a honing beacon, like a magnet — and zero right in on the thing inside you that got activated.

Then, in almost zero time, you can deal with it: embrace it, bring it up into the heart space, feel it, then let it go, throw it in the fire, whatever. All while you're watching the flick. You're multi-tasking — got two levels of consciousness working at the same time: watching the movie, and playing the game, making issues conscious.

Like this: "Whoa! I'm angry in that scene: when he does that to her. Dude, I know this anger — totally familiar. So, here I go, inside, on the vertical, like an elevator down into my life. Yeah, reminds me of when I was in school, and those bullies were picking on that innocent girl. Come to think of it, my daddy used to be like that to my little sister." See what I mean? Follow the feeling. Ride the lightning. That way you don't get left holding the bag. You turned that situation around, made it work for you. Instead of being a victim of the movie, the movie's your ally.

Even if all this is brand new to you, and it works best to play it like we outlined it above, when you get more used to it, this is the way you'll be able to do it, too. What's beautiful is, after a while, Movie Yoga will become like second nature — just as easy as breathing. This is when we really get cruising into a new way of living: clear and clean on the inside, running light, no excess baggage dragging us down, bright-eyed and wide open on the outside. A whole new world, and worth it.

CHAPTER 14: LIVING IN THE MYSTERY

Cypher: *I know what you're thinking, 'cause right now I'm thinking the same thing. Actually, I've been thinking it ever since I got here. Why oh why didn't I take the BLUE pill?"*

~ *The Matrix*

Craig Schwartz, on the existence of a portal into John Malkovich's head: *The point is, this is a very odd thing, supernatural, for lack of a better word. It raises all sorts of philosophical questions about the nature of self, about the existence of the soul. Am I me? Is Malkovich Malkovich? Was the Buddha right? Is duality an illusion? Do you see what a can of worms this portal is? I don't think I can go on living my life as I have lived it. There's only one thing left to do. Let's get married right away.*

~ *Being John Malkovich*

HAL 9000: *Dave, my mind is going. I can feel it.*

~ *2001: A Space Odyssey*

Galadriel: *And to you Frodo Baggins, I give the light of Earendil, our most beloved star. May it be a light for you in dark places, when all other lights go out.*

~ *Lord of the RIngs: The Fellowship of the Ring*

To Believe in This Living Is Just a Hard Way to Go

I want to touch on something here about the on-going nature of doing this kind of Movie Yoga practice in our lives. It's possible that a movie, or any outside event, can trigger something that's pretty overwhelming. It could be that we're seeing the event or pattern for the first time, in which case the feelings may be unexpected and quite powerful. This could be because of some childhood trauma, or even something from our birth. We may have known this issue existed, but this time it comes up in a much stronger way than before.

If this happens, it might not be so easy to just let it go. We may actually try to, but the pattern could be so intense that it hangs on. We continue, off and on, to experience the powerful emotions associated with it. This can be tough. We can even feel as though we're doing Movie Yoga all wrong. But the fact is, we're actually doing it really well. It means that the Inner Healer is working for us, bringing things into our awareness, so we have more opportunities to work with them. It's just that, before we're able to let the pattern go, sometimes something else has to happen first. And this has to do with what we've covered a lot: the fact that, one: the Inner Healer is in charge of our growth and, two: consciousness or awareness is how healing happens.

So, let's think this scenario through — the one where something powerful has come up, it's blindsided us, and we feel we can't just let it go very easily. So, let's do the drill: When the pattern emerges, it's being brought into our awareness by the Inner Healer via our Awareness Positioning System™. This much we know. So far, so good. But the Inner Healer is not only in charge of bringing it into our awareness, it's also in charge of how long it's going to take before it's healed. It would be wonderful if every pattern we had would just come up, and then would instantly disappear. But that's not how it always works.

Some patterns just plain have a lot of power in our lives — more than we could imagine. There may even be some traumas that have affected what feels like the very core of our beings. Then we're going to have a lot of beads on that particular string; we will have been through a lot of tough times that seem to be connected to one of these early traumas. So, it's reasonable that these kinds of patterns are just going to take some time to heal. They will take a lot of awareness and consciousness. It'll probably take some serious systematic effort, like therapy, meditation, prayer, and so on, in order for us to truly get acquainted with these patterns fully, own them, and then ultimately release them so that we can feel better.

Just about any of us who have been doing any of these kinds of systematic practices over the years will admit that some of our patterns are just plain stubborn. They've been around a long time, and it feels like we have a ton of energy in them. It can begin to be kind of laughable how we keep getting the same triggers from movies that we watch, over and over again. Feelings and patterns don't go belly up just because we look at them once or twice, or even ten or twenty times.

We've already gone through some strategies — like meditation, therapy, prayer, dance, etc. — that can be our allies as we're working with what's come up for us when we play Movie Yoga. But I'd like to mention one more that I and many of my fellow Movie Yogis have been using for years and which we swear by as one of the surest roads to transformation.* This practice uses really simple deep breathing to create a situation where we can listen to some intense music, go into a sort of waking, deep trance state, and stay in it for two to three hours.

While in this state, we can have all kinds of experiences. We get in touch with deep feelings, release physical tensions and blockages in the body, have spiritual breakthroughs, and work through traumas — even ones we didn't know about consciously until they came up, like at a movie when we were playing Movie Yoga. We can also get all kinds of insights and understandings about humanity, the world, and the cosmos that are rarely available in the ordinary waking state — everything from the smallest regret all the way to cosmic consciousness.

Afterwards, the experience often leads to feelings of real freedom, healing, and release. We don't do this breathing practice on our own, but have somebody there just to support us as we go through these inner journeys. What's cool is that, when we support each other like this, we basically just try to stay out of the way of the ones doing the breathing so they can experience the journey fully and uninterrupted. Most of us who do it feel it's been incredibly positive and life changing. And one of the most profound things about it is that we discover the power of our own Inner Healer inside us — and that there's no great expert outside us making healing happen. Totally empowering.

But there's more good news too. What we always find is that, if we do Movie Yoga consistently, with the help of the practices we've been talking about, our patterns, even the really tough ones, bother us less and less over time. And we are able to lead much more fulfilling lives, without being controlled by the things that used to bother us a lot. Our leashes get longer and longer, meaning we get more and more empowerment and freedom in our lives. The practice works. It's just not always an instant cure. But let me know when you find a quick fix that is fool proof. I'll be the first to sign up.

---

* Holotropic Breathwork™

The Light of Earendil

Let's take a quick return trip to Shelob's Lair. You remember, Frodo in the birth canal, the tunnel, running from the monster spider, getting all strung up in the Trapped Zone. Well, something else happened in there I didn't mention, but seems totally relevant, now that we're touching on how tough transformation can be sometimes. When Shelob was closing in, Frodo had a flash and remembered something he had forgotten up 'til now, maybe because he didn't need it before. He pulls a crystal vial of clear liquid out of his pocket. It's a gift from Galadriel, Queen of the Elves.

And she tells him what you may have just read — one of the quotes at the beginning of this chapter: "And for you, Frodo Baggins. I give you the light of Earendil, our most beloved star. May it be a light for you in the dark places, when all other lights go out."

You better believe all those lights had gone out for him, there, deep under the mountains of Mordor. So what do you reckon he was expecting from this gift, when he pulls it out and recites the magic words? Like, some bad-ass creature ally was going to pop out of the bottle like a ninja genie and open up a can of whatever on Shelob? Maybe an elvin army? Probably. Something like that. At least that's what he was hoping for.

Well, what happened? The cave got lit up, that's what. Bright enough for him to see what was about to tear him apart. No ninja, no ray of power, no magic potion aerosol spraying out and burning up Shelob, like water melted the Wicked Witch of the West in The Wizard of Oz. *Just light. That's all. In* Bladerunner, *the replicant Roy Battie, whose four-year life span was over, is having a face-to-face with his maker, Dr. Elden Tyrell. Tyrell says he can't help him with this life span thing, but would he want to be modified in some way. Roy replies, "Had in mind something a little more radical. I want more life, Father."*

Maybe Frodo had in mind something a little more radical too. Light was all he got. Is that all? Going to hit Shelob with the light? But you know what? In Movie Yoga, light's just about everything. What would have happened to Frodo if the cave had not *gotten lit up? He wouldn't have seen Shelob, and she would have eaten him, or worse. He wouldn't have been able to draw his sword, Sting, and face her, fight back, do what was necessary to continue his quest.*

Okay, what's light to us in Movie Yoga? I'm talking about the light of awareness, the light of consciousness. The greatest gift of healing we have, the true power of our Inner Healer.

So here's what this movie episode means for us: When we embark on the epic journey of discovering ourselves, we're just like Frodo — deep in the darkness of our own unconscious, under the weight of the mountain of our past. We're looking for a way through. We're on a quest. When we uncover something that feels too painful, we may just look for a way out. But somehow we know the only way out is through.

But, just like Frodo, we've been given an ally: light — our awareness itself. But, armed with this ally of awareness, what do we think will happen? That we'll just start cruising, ease on down the road, no worries? That when we uncover some pattern or feeling, like getting triggered in a movie, and we trace it back, it's just going to disappear, like poof, like magic? Sorry, but most of the time, that's not how it works. It's usually a little more intense than that.

When we first get in touch with something, especially if it's a rough one, I have to admit, it can sorta feel like we've been cheated. We pull out the elixir, the gift from our own inner Galadriel, our Higher Self, or whatever our source of inspiration is. Consciousness, the light, that's the gift. But instead of healing us right away, killing the Shelobs that haunt the caves of our past, what does the light do? Like with Frodo, it reveals to us the worst thing we can imagine. It doesn't destroy it. It just points it out, shows us what's there, brings the light of awareness to it. Gives us a blueprint of what we have to do next with this issue we just found.

Feels a bit diabolical, right? I know. Talk about getting led into the forest. No operation manual, that kind of thing. But this is the way transformation works most of the time. No quick fixes, very few deus ex machinas, *just a real rare magic bullet now and then. But we're not in a tragedy, just an adventure. We've all got our Stings — the strategies we've learned that'll show us what to do with whatever our lights of Earendil have revealed to us. We're not empty-handed.*

Are we willing to make friends with the light? Because this is the only way we're going to get through our personal Mordors. Yeah, I know, that first big awakening of feelings can sometimes come as a nasty surprise. And this is going to sound a little tough. But you know what, we're just going to have to cowboy and cowgirl up. Hey, we're just adding a fresh nuance to the phrase, 'lighten up'. You got it, we have to lighten up. Fill ourselves with the light of consciousness.

> *This is how we heal. It may not have been what we were looking for. But how many times have we gotten something different from what we expected and it turned out to be the perfect gift, even though at the time it'd have been the last thing we thought we needed? Well, here it is again: the light of Earendil, our own special gift. Now all we gotta do is use it, when all other lights go out, in the dark places of our own psyches. The perfect gift at the perfect time, if we can learn to trust it.*

When We Get Blinded by the Light

Remember when we asked ourselves the question of whether we were being motivated by our past, drawn back by our feelings into a very real or imagined perfection that may have existed at one time? Or whether, in fact, we were being spurred on by something in our future, pulled forward, as if by a beacon from a lighthouse way out there that somehow contains a future blueprint of our perfection that we are growing into? You might also recall how we decided that both were true. We seem to need to do both in order to really feel fulfilled.

Well, asking ourselves those two questions we explored — one, "Is this familiar?" and two, "Have I ever felt this before?" — covers the first half of this dynamic (the part about needing to get in touch with those things from the past that have motivated us to act in rigid patterns over and over again, which assures that we'll repeat the same mistakes again and again.)

But what about the lighthouse out there in our future? What happens when we get rocked by something totally unfamiliar? Something that, when we ask, "Is this familiar?" and "Have I ever felt this before?" the answer comes up, nope, and nope again. Never felt it. Haven't got a clue.

This is what I call getting blind-sided, hit from the side where we weren't looking. You might also remember my mentioning that we tend to grow in two ways. One is a gradual kind of awakening that takes place over a period of time. You know, like we go to therapy for a month or two, and it may seem like a waste, because nothing much is happening. Or maybe we started a yoga or a meditation class, and truth be told, it's actually been mostly just boring.

And then one day we wake up, and we notice that we feel just a little bit different, better in a subtle way. Something we couldn't pick up on in the short run, but which is gradually emerging as some kind of lasting, perhaps bedrock foundation that we think we can actually begin to build a whole new life upon.

Our bodies are just a little less tense. We aren't reacting with anger quite as quickly as we used to. These kinds of changes are essential, but they're not going to blow us out of the water. Not too many bells and whistles on them, just a kind of every-day, ho-hum, my life is changing, but where's the beef kind of thing.

Okay, but what about the other kind of growth, such as the examples I've shared that happened to me in the theater — with *Bladerunner* or *Apocalypse Now* or *Fantasia* — ones like that? Oh boy, here's where we get blown open, rocked. So, you're one of those who's always looking for the fireworks? Kind of have to be hit over the head? Nothing wrong with that. Mystical literature is filled with these kinds of experiences. In fact, that's how every meaningful philosophy or movement got started — somebody got blown open.

Like I said, more power to you. Except for one little, itsy bitsy thing: there is no way we're going to be ready for these kinds of experiences. Because they are by nature rule-busting, mind-shattering, veil-parting, mold-cracking, risk-taking, dream-changing, attitude-destroying, question-asking, bright-eyed, open-mouthed, head-spinning, sleep-losing, knee-knocking, heart-thumping, run-from, crawl-toward life-changers. But besides that, there's nothing much to worry about.

The reason there's nothing to worry about is because, when they do happen to us — and believe me, at some point they will — we're going to be like the Bob Dylan character from *Blood on the Tracks*. Just when we're absolutely convinced we're "poisoned in the bushes and blown out on the trail," some beautiful, compassionate power that is a total mystery to us will say, "Come in, I'll give you shelter from the storm."

And just what is that shelter from the storm of confusion, of being born anew in this world with, as Buckminster Fuller would say, no operation manual for spaceship Earth? This is when a whole new world will open up before us — of experiences, of just the right people showing up. The book that falls off the shelf and hits us in the head. The movie a friend turns us on to that we've been avoiding. The new job, the pilgrimage into nature, the smile on the bus, the light on the path — these events and countless more, big and small, yet all of them meaningful.

Because what comes with transformation is mainly just waking up, paying attention, seeing and feeling what we missed before. And the amazing discovery is that the storm of transformation, and the shelter from it, are there all around us, always have been. We just weren't paying attention.

Like I said before, if we play Movie Yoga, we'll never see movies the same way again. But I'll take it even one step further. What's an even more profound gift is that, when these kinds of experiences begin to happen for us in any of the miracle ways they can, we'll never experience life the same way again either. That's the big secret that ain't no big secret.

That's why we play Movie Yoga. It'll be why, if you do play it and dig it, you'll one day go, "Hey, you know what? This game will work for relationship too. And, oh yeah, it's perfect for raising kids. And going to work. And oh, wait a minute, it'll even work for cutting the bread, and picking the flowers, and making love, and saving the planet. And, now that I think about it, everything, the whole trip, is a *yoga*."

"If I can stay just a little more awake, pay just a little bit more attention, there's absolutely no telling what life's going to reveal, what epic adventures might be in store for me."

Come to think of it, that'd actually be a pretty good turn-around on a not-too-intense investment in what, at the time, seemed like nothing but a game.

And we thought we were just going to watch some movies.

Welcome to "Life Yoga". Embrace. Enjoy.

EPILOGUE: SUNSHINE

Ricky Fitts: *It was one of those days when it's a minute away from snowing, and there's this electricity in the air, you can almost hear it, right? And this bag was, like, dancing with me. Like a little kid begging for me to play with it. For fifteen minutes. And that's the day I knew there was this entire life behind things, and... this incredibly benevolent force that wanted me to know there was no reason to be afraid, ever. Video's a poor excuse. But it helps me to remember... and I need to remember... Sometimes there's so much beauty in the world I feel like I can't take it, like my heart's going to cave in.*

~ American Beauty

Frodo: *My dear Sam. You cannot always be torn in two. You will have to be one and whole for many years. You have so much to enjoy and to be and to do. Your part in the story will go on.*

~ Lord of the Rings: The Return of the King

I. H. McDunnough: *But still I hadn't dreamed nothin' about me and Ed — until the end. And this was cloudier, because it was years, years away. But I saw an old couple being visited by their children, and all their grandchildren too. The grandcouple wasn't screwed up, and neither was the kids, or their grandkids. And, I don't know — you tell me — that it's all a dream. Was it wishful thinking? Was I just fleeing reality like I know I'm liable to do? But, me and Ed, we can be good too. And it seemed real. And it seemed like us and it seemed like — well, our home. If not Arizona, then a land not too far away. Where all parents are strong and wise and capable. And all children are happy and beloved. I don't know — maybe it was Utah.*

~ Raising Arizona

Epilogue: Sunshine

Bryn and I just saw *Sunshine* — what was maybe my favorite movie of that year — in the top five anyway. (On our DLP — our poor person's plasma. I'm not complaining. We are lucky if, every movie we watch, the house doesn't come down around us, the sofa, the TV, and the sound system. Got 'outlaw' bass.)

Sunshine's another masterpiece from Danny Boyle, written by Alex Garland: The sun is dying. And thus, the earth. A group of young astronauts and scientists are flying a bomb the size of Manhattan into the sun, with the hopes of re-igniting it. The project has taken all the resources left on the planet. Last shot. It's turning out to be a one-way mission, even if they ever get that close.

Sounds goofy, right? It's not. It's awesome: terrifying, haunting, epic, gorgeous, nail-biting, sweet, heart-wrenching, and absolutely cool. How am I going to end this book, when movies like this one keep opening my heart? The last few years definitely has their share of masterpieces: *Pan's Labyrinth*, *The Fountain*, *Children of Men*, *Rescue Dawn*, *3:10 to Yuma*, *No Country for Old Men*, *There Will Be Blood*, *300*, *Lars and the Real Girl*, *American Gangster*, *Eastern Promises*, *The Dark Knight*, *Slum Dog Millionaire*, *In Bruges*, *The Reader*, *Revolutionary Road*, *Watchmen*, and that's just a few. I know, these are my few. Thanks for humoring me this far.

We're told that gratitude is a power — just feeling it can change us in a bigtime positive way. I believe it. I feel so blessed to be able to walk out of the theater, or get up off my sofa, so full of feelings that I'm often vulnerable, like a child. So emptied out of knowledge; instead, I'm so full of wonder, so not knowing, so in awe of a mystery much greater than myself. To be able to experience passion and the power of creation over and over, the way the techno-mystery of movies pours through us, in what I truly believe is one of the greatest art forms of this age — well, it's fulfilling. What else can I say?

This art form doesn't have to be your gig. Far from it. But all of our gigs, if there's passion enough in them, can maybe help light a fire in us. Sometimes I wish I had a staff, like Gandalf, or a magic wand, like Harry Potter. But, you know what? If I did, I'd screw it up.

One of the characters in *Sunshine* says, right before he sacrifices himself for his crew, and lets the sun incinerate him, "We're nothing but stardust." Nothing but stardust. Is that all? Not too shabby, stardust. Which, incidentally, was a pretty magical movie too. In *Stardust*, there's this... here I go again. Like I already said, somebody stop me.

But in *Sunshine*, you know what that star-farer does when he's just seconds before the sun burns him up? He puts on the darkest shades he has, and goes up on the observation deck, and waits for the ship to rotate around 'til the sun's not obstructed by the shield. And then he just stares right at it, eyes wide open, soul wide open, checking out light for as long as he can, surrendering to death. And then, I'm betting he finds out he was right. Nothing but stardust. But what's my point? Does it matter? No. What matters is that, in this moment, because of *Sunshine*, I feel closer to something marvelous than I did a few hours before. Who could ask for more?

Appendix A

MOVIES FOR MOVIE YOGA

Here are the films I mention or explore in *Movie Yoga*. Keep in mind, this is just a one constellation in the universe of films, all of which are good to play Movie Yoga with.

2001: A Space Odyssey
20,000 Leagues Under the Sea
The Abyss
AI - Artificial Intelligence
Alien
Aliens
Aliens of the Deep
Alien 3
Alien Resurrection
Angels in America
Badlands
Bambi
Batman Begins
Bladerunner
Blood of Dracula
Blueberry (or Renegade)
Blade trilogy
Bonnie and Clyde
Bram Stoker's Dracula
Braveheart
Brubaker
Cabeza de Vaca
Casualties of War
City of Lost Children
Cold Mountain
Cool Hand Luke
The Crow
Dark City
Days of Heaven
El Mariachi
Elvira Madigan
Equus
Fantasia
Fifty First Dates
Finding Nemo
A Fistful of Dollars
For a Few Dollars More
Gallipoli
Gladiator
The Godfather trilogy
Gone with the Wind
The Good, the Bad, and the Ugly
The Great Escape
Harry Potter Series
Igby Goes Down
In Bruges
Indiana Jones and the Temple of Doom

I Was a Teenage Frankenstein
Jacob's Ladder
Jaws
Kill Bill I and *Kill Bill II*
Kingdom of Heaven
Kundun
The Last Temptation of Christ
Lawrence of Arabia
The Lord of the Rings: The Fellowship of the Ring
The Lord of the Rings: The Two Towers
The Lord of the Rings: The Return of the King
Love Actually
The Magdalene Sisters
The Matrix
Memento
Metropolis
The Mission
The Mummy
Old Yeller
The Omen
Once Upon a Time in America
One Flew Over the Cuckoo's Nest
Ordinary People
The Passion of the Christ
Platoon
Poltergeist
Pride and Prejudice
Princess Mononoke
Psycho
Pulp Fiction
The Reader
Revolutionary Road
Road to Perdition
Road Warrior trilogy
Romy and Michelle's High School Reunion
Room with a View
Saving Private Ryan
Se7en
Seventh Voyage of Sinbad
The Shawshank Redemption
Slum Dog Millionaire
Spirited Away
The Squid and the Whale
Star Wars
Terminator
Terms of Endearment
Thief
The Thin Red Line
Training Day
Watchmen
Wizard of Oz
Wolf Creek

Appendix B

EXAMPLES USED IN *MOVIE YOGA*

Here's the list of movies I used in *Movie Yoga* as examples of the Death/Rebirth Matrix. If the "start of segment" column is blank, the segment begins at the beginning of the chapter. If it doesn't, I give the time in hours, minutes, and seconds where the clip is located in the disc chapter. Happy playing!

Film Title	Chapter	Start of Segment	Length of Segment
THE SAFE ZONE			
Finding Nemo	4		1 min 20 sec
The Beach	11		2 min 30 sec
The Thin Red Line	1	0:1:07	2 min 53 sec
THE SAFE ZONE-TOXIC WOMB			
Jaws	2	0:2:00	50 sec
Poltergeist	41	1:42:20	1 min 25 sec

Film Title	Chapter	Start of Segment	Length of Segment
THE SAFE ZONE			
Finding Nemo	4		1 min 20 sec
The Beach	11		2 min 30 sec
The Thin Red Line	1	0:1:07	2 min 53 sec
THE SAFE ZONE-TOXIC WOMB			
Jaws	2	0:2:00	50 sec
Poltergeist	41	1:42:20	1 min 25 sec

Film Title	Chapter	Start of Segment	Length of Segment
THE TRAPPED ZONE			
Star Wars	34		4 min 45 min
AI: Artificial Intelligence	13	0:48:30	33 min 8 sec
Jacob's Ladder	27	1:14:22	1 min 52 sec
Metropolis	3	9:44	4 min
LOTR: The Return of the King (extended)	2	0:1:00	6 min 12 sec
THE WAR ZONE			
Gladiator	2	0:7:15	5 min
Pulp Fiction	11		4 min
Bram Stoker's Dracula	14		2 min 30 sec

APPENDIX B - EXAMPLES USED IN *MOVIE YOGA*

Film Title	Chapter	Start of Segment	Length of Segment
THE FREE ZONE			
The Shawshank Redemption	32	1:58:28	2 min
The Abyss	39	2:03:00	4 min
The Mission	11	0:39:48	2 min 41 sec
Fantasia	15	1:50:00	14 min
LOTR: The Return of the King	72		3 min 40 sec
Renegade	21 & 22		10 min

INDEX

12 Steps, 18, 162
20,000 Leagues under the Sea, 181
2001: A Space Odyssey, 142, 170, 181
28 Days, 47
3:10 to Yuma, 179
300, 60, 69, 110, 114, 179
A Fistful of Dollars, 82, 181
abandonment, 44-45, 100
abuse, 27, 81, 91
Abyss, The, 142, 181, 186
action movie, 57
addiction, 18, 40, 81, 84, 110-111, 140, 141
aggression, 48, 68, 110-111, 117-118
AI: Artificial Intelligence, 132, 181, 185
Alamo, The, 28, 60, 113
alchemy, 14, 155
Alcoholics Anonymous, 18, 39, 104, 162
Alien movies, 21, 59-60, 119-121, 123-124, 133, 142, 164, 181, 185
Allman Brothers, 47-48
aloneness, 27, 83, 95, 98, 100, 132, 156
American Beauty, 178
American Gangster, 179
amniotic universe, 87, 156
anesthesia, 130
Angels in America, 82, 181
anger, 25, 42-44, 111, 115, 132, 161, 168, 175
apocalypse, 19, 80, 122, 124, 126, 130, 133, 176
Apocalypse Now, 19, 124, 126, 133, 176, 185
APS™, 6, 33-43, 45, 58-59, 62-63, 72, 76, 124, 160, 165, 168
archetype, 15, 28, 43, 58, 61, 63, 71, 81, 83-85, 89, 92, 98, 100, 102, 106, 114, 117, 119, 124, 126-127, 134, 138, 145, 155-156
Arrien, Angeles, 29
Ason, *see* Sparks, Ason
Attack of the Killer Tomatoes, 109
Awareness Positioning System™, 6, 33-43, 45, 58-59, 62-63, 72, 76, 124, 160, 165, 168

awareness, meta-level, 35
Baghavad Gita, 122
Bambi, 27, 64, 181
Batman Begins, 120, 181
Battie, Roy, 17, 21, 104, 124, 173
Beach, The, 78, 84, 87-88, 92, 132, 184
Being John Malkovich, 170
Being There, 78
Ben Hur, 28, 82
Bergman, Ingmar, 111
birth, 19, 48, 50, 58, 61, 66, 76-77, 79-81, 83-84, 87, 91-93, 95-98, 102-103, 106-107, 111, 117, 122-123, 128, 130, 132, 135, 137-138, 143-144, 171, 173
, anesthesia in, 130
, biological, 76-77
birth canal, 48, 58, 84, 96, 106, 111, 128, 137-138, 143, 173, *see also* tunnel
Blade, 120, 181
Bladerunner, 12, 17-18, 20-22, 28, 65, 104-105, 120, 124, 129, 173, 176, 181
blame, 43-44
Blood of Dracula, 28, 181
Blood on the Tracks, 176
Blueberry, See Renegade
Bonnie and Clyde, 65, 181
Boyle, Danny, 84, 87, 142, 179
Brahman, 19
Bram Stoker's Dracula, 118, 133, 181, 185
Braveheart, 82, 114, 181
Bridge on the River Kwai, 28
Brubaker, 181
Buddhism, 37-38, 149, 162-163, 170
Caan, James, 112
Cabeza de Vaca, 31, 181
Call to Adventure, the, 49, 79, 83, 132, 159
Cameron, James, 21, 65, 119-120, 142, 144
Campbell, Joseph, 14, 48, 79, 128, 153
Captains Courageous, 27
Casualties of War, 82, 181
Cat People, 109
catharsis, 25-26, 71, 98, 139
Caviezel, Jim, 91-92

INDEX

Chariots of Fire, 159
Children of Men, 75, 95, 179
City of Lost Children, 120, 181
Clash of the Titans, 30
Clean and Sober, 47
Coen brothers, 33
Cold Mountain, 114, 181
collective unconscious, 28, 48, 81, 136, 141
comedy, 38, 54, 68, 98, 130
Conrad, Joseph, 124
Contact, 21
Cool Hand Luke, 97, 181
Coppola, Francis Ford, 118, 120, 124, 127
courage, 16, 30, 63, 132, 161
Cronenweth, Jordan, 19
Crouching Tiger, Hidden Dragon, 52
Crow, The, 69, 181
Crowe, Russell, 24, 70, 113
Dalai Lama, 133
Daltry, Roger, 138
Dances with Wolves, 159
danger, 80, 83, 91, 93, 96, 119, 130, 132
Darabont, Frank, 137
Dark City, 69, 181
Dark Knight, 60, 120, 179
Dark Side, the, 28, 61, 117-118
Davy Crockett, 28
Days of Heaven, 88, 181
De Niro, Robert, 139
De Palma, Brian, 82
death, 20-21, 26-29, 31-32, 46, 49-50, 57-61, 65, 70-71, 76-77, 79, 81, 8-84, 91, 92, 94-95, 98, 100-104, 107-108, 111, 114, 116-119, 122-123, 127-136, 140-144, 146, 148-150, 152-154, 180
, ego, 131, 140
, fear of, 104
, metaphorical, 131
death/rebirth, 26-27, 32, 50, 77, 100
Death/Rebirth Matrix, 6, 33-35, 47-48, 50-51, 75-77, 80, 99, 184
, chart of the, 80
Del Toro, Guillermo, 105, 120
demons, 101, 110, 117-118, 151, 154
depression, 13, 38, 49, 80, 85, 95, 110, 149
Desperado, 109
Di Caprio, Leonardo, 84-85
Dionysus, 102
Douglas, Kirk, 43
Dr. Zhivago, 82

Dracula, 118-119, 185
dream, 27, 29, 50, 85-87, 102, 107-108, 117-119, 146, 178
Dylan, Bob, 176
Eastern Promises, 179
ecstasy, 80, 89, 105, 137, 148, 151, 161, 165
El Mariachi, 14, 109, 181
Elvira Madigan, 65, 181
epic, 22, 26- 48, 52, 54, 66, 82, 85, 89, 92, 99, 110, 112, 114, 120, 122, 134, 142-43, 150, 154, 174, 177, 179
Equus, 31, 181
evil, 15, 58, 61-2, 64, 80, 91, 107, 126-28, 154
false self, 21, 122-123, 131-132, 134, 140-141, 149
Fancher, Hampton, 19
Fantasia, 28, 117-118, 150-151, 176, 181, 186
fear, 28, 37, 57, 59-61, 68, 81, 83, 95, 104, 107-109, 128, 147, 149, 161
Fellini, Frederico, 95
Fellowship of the Ring, 16, 68, 75, 105, 107, 112, 170, 173-175, 182, *see also Lord of the Rings* trilogy
Feminine, the, 58, 155-156
fetus, 48, 79, 93, 95, 103, 110, 115, 128, 130, 135
Fifty First Dates, 70, 181
Fight Club, 30, 129
filmmaker, 5, 26, 88-90, 98, 102, 114, 137, 151, 153
Fincher, David, 58, 120
Finding Nemo, 63, 81, 83, 92, 132, 181, 184
Finding Neverland, 78
Firth, Colin, 70
For a Few Dollars More, 82, 181
Ford, Harrison, 18, 104
Fountain, The, 129, 135, 179
Free Zone, the, 6, 35, 46, 50, 76, 79-81, 86, 87, 108, 111, 117, 121, 123, 126, 131, 135-156
freedom, 36-37, 65, 68, 80, 87, 90, 97, 134-136, 138, 140, 144, 154, 172
Freeman, Morgan, 137
Freud, Sigmund, 48, 131
Frodo, 22, 75, 106-108, 132, 145-149, 167, 170, 173-174, 178
Fuller, Buckminster, 100, 176
Gaghan, Stephen, 89

Gallipoli, 24, 65, 181
Garland, Alex, 84, 87, 179
Gibson, Mel, 91, 114
Giger, H. R., 120
Gladiator, 24, 70, 78, 82, 94, 112-114, 129, 132, 182, 185
Glass, Philip, 133
global crisis, 141
Godfather, The, 120, 124, 182
Gone with the Wind, 28, 82, 182
Grant, Hugh, 70
Great Escape, The, 97, 182
Great Mother, 19
Grof, Stanislav, 5, 46, 77
Groundhog Day, 94
guilt, 66, 99, 139, 140
Hanged Man, the, 102
Hanks, Tom, 77
Hannibal, 103, 109
Harris, Ed, 142-143
Harry Potter, 120, 179, 182
Hauer, Rutger, 104
Hawke, Ethan, 34
healing, 31, 36, 41, 53, 57, 67, 99-100, 124, 161-162, 171, 174
Heart of Darkness, The, 124
heaven, 14, 18-19, 22, 52, 79, 83-87, 91, 93, 95, 98, 100-102, 105, 107, 132, 149, 151, 156
hell, 13-14, 22, 27, 29, 45, 57, 59, 62-63, 82-83, 86, 93, 95, 100-102, 104, 107, 110, 114-115, 121-122, 125, 130, 132, 145, 149
Hellboy, 105, 120
hero, 12, 25, 29, 43, 57, 71, 84, 89, 102-104, 108, 120, 126, 145-146, 149, 154-156
Hero's Journey, the, 49, 79, 95-96, 101, 103, 110-111, 115, 130
Higher Power, 162, 167
Hobbit, The, 105, 120
Hollywood, 14, 20, 27, 55, 57, 88-90, 111, 120, 136
Holotropic Breathwork™, 172
honor, 29, 70-71
Hooper, Tobe, 93
hopelessness, 95, 104-105, 110, 145
horror movies, 38, 54, 58-60, 62, 93, 98, 107, 120, 132
Hurricane, 135
Hutton, Timothy, 63

I Was a Teenage Frankenstein, 28, 182
Igby Goes Down, 63, 182
In Bruges, 179, 182
Indiana Jones and the Temple of Doom, 97, 182
Industrial Light and Magic, 19
Inner Healer, 36, 38, 41, 58, 62, 124-125, 161-162, 164, 171-173
innocence, 79, 83, 91-92, 136, 148, 155
insane asylum, 97, 101-102, 137
Jackson, Peter, 18, 22, 31, 105, 114, 120, 136
Jacob's Ladder, 101, 132, 182, 185
Jaws, 26, 28, 59, 92, 132, 182, 184
Joffe, Roland, 139
Jung, Carl, 28, 49, 67, 81, 117, 126, 131, 150
Kali, 121
Kill Bill, 69, 182
Kingdom of Heaven, 114, 182
Kubrick, Stanley, 142
Kumbha Mela, 20
Kundun, 133, 182, 185
Kurosawa, Akira, 114
Lang, Fritz, 102
Lars and the Real Girl, 63, 179
Last Temptation of Christ, The, 133, 182
Lawrence of Arabia, 82, 114, 182
Lean, David, 114
Leaving Las Vegas, 47
Legends of the Fall, 30
Leone, Sergio, 82
Lewis, Juliet, 155
Lord of the Rings trilogy, 12, 16, 31-32, 59, 68, 75, 82, 89-90, 94, 105-107, 112, 114, 144, 147, 150, 170, 173-175, 182, 185-186
love, 13, 15, 18, 25, 37, 43, 54, 59, 62, 65-66, 68, 79, 81, 83, 87, 89, 91, 99, 109, 119, 130, 140, 144, 147-148, 155-156, 161, 177
Love Actually, 70, 182
Lovecraft, H. P., 151
Lucas, George, 79, 96-97
Magdelene Sisters, The, 63, 182
Malick, Terrence, 65, 88-92, 114
Mann, Michael, 112
Masculine, the, 155
Matrix, The, 65, 69, 85, 99, 168, 170, 182
McGregor, Ewen, 84

INDEX

meditation, 14, 16, 28, 35, 153, 162, 167-168, 171-172, 175
Meet Joe Black, 82
Memento, 89, 182
Merchant/Ivory, 70
metalevel awareness, 35
Metropolis, 102, 104-105, 132, 182, 185
Milius, John, 124
Miller, George, 120
Miller's Crossing, 33
Minghella, Anthony, 114
Mission, The, 139-141, 182, 186
Miyazaki, Hayao, 90
Moby, 86
Moby Dick, 26
monster, 21, 63, 107-108, 123, 173
Moody Blues, 127
Morricone, Ennio, 82, 139
Morrison, Jim, 155
Mother Nature, 32, 92
Mother, the Divine, 79-80, 156
mother
 , protective, 122
 , separation from the, 99
Mount Doom, 16, 107, 145-148
movie
 , how to listen to a, 82
 , how to 'eat' a, 90
 , looks in a, 112
 , sequels to a, 120
Movie Yoga
 , emotional survey for playing, 164-168
 , for couples, 69-72
 , game of, 31, 50, 144, 160
 , how to play, 32-37
 , map for playing, 26
 , short form for playing, 35, 76
 , Zones in, 51
  see also Safe Zone, Trapped Zone, War Zone, Free Zone, Death/Rebirth Matrix
Movie Yogi, 55-57, 59, 62-63
movie, favorite, 105
movies as ritual, 126
movies,
 , adventure, 119
 , comedy, 38, 54, 68, 98, 130
 , crying at, 17, 64-65, 98, 107, 111, 137, 147
 , epic, 86, 91, 151, *see also* epic
 , horror, 38, 54, 58-60, 62, 93, 98, 107, 120, 132
 , Japanese, 90
 , sci-fi, 18, 54, 120-121
 , violent, 66-67
 , war, 151
 , Westerns, 90, 153-154
movies we don't like, 57-64
Mummy, The, 28, 182
Mussorgsky, Modest, 151
Mystery School, 50
Mystery, the, 20, 91, 143, 170-177
myth, 43, 75, 102, 121, 123
Newman, Thomas, 81-82, 137
New World, The, 78, 88, 135
Nicholson, Jack, 65
Nip/Tuck, 27
No Country for Old Men, 179
Nolan, Christopher, 89, 120
Oakley, Berry, 47-48
ocean, 87
oceanic ecstasy, 92
Old Yeller, 27, 64-65, 182
Oldman, Gary, 118
Omen, The, 61, 182
Once Upon a Time in America, 82, 182
One Flew Over the Cuckoo's Nest, 65, 97, 182
Ordinary People, 63-64, 182
Orpheus, 102
Oscar, 55, 62, 70, 120, 153
Osiris, 102
Oz, 97
pain, 25, 27, 40, 42, 63-64, 68, 71, 79-81, 84, 87, 94-95, 98-101, 132, 138-140, 144, 148-149
Paltrow, Gwyneth, 58
Pan's Labyrinth, 46, 105, 179
paradise, 78, 83, 85, 91-92, 155
Passion of the Christ, The, 91, 182
Peckinpah, Sam, 82, 114
Pee Wee's Big Adventure, 94
Peoples, David, 19
perfection, 85-88, 106-107, 132, 175
phoenix, 123
Phoenix, Joaquin, 70
Piano, The, 82, 129
Pippin, 16, 129
Platoon, 114, 182

Poe, Edgar Allen, 151
Poltergeist, 93, 96, 182, 184
powerlessness, 95, 97, 111
prayer, 35, 162, 167, 171-172
Pride and Prejudice, 70, 182
Princess Mononoke, 90, 182
prison, 97, 135, 137-138
psyche, 5, 29, 47-48, 50, 59, 61, 81, 90-91, 106, 112, 119, 123-124, 131, 134, 136, 141-142, 149, 151, 175
Psycho, 28, 182
Pulp Fiction, 69, 115-117, 119, 132, 182, 185
'pyrocatharsis', 122, 148, 162
rage, 80, 110, 145
Raimi, Sam, 120
Raising Arizona, 178
Ran, 114
Reader, The, 179, 182
rebirth, 6, 11, 25-26, 28-29, 31-35, 46-47, 49-50, 61, 64-65, 75-77, 79-81, 83-84, 91-92, 99-102, 104, 111, 114, 117-118, 122-123, 126-128, 131-132, 134-141, 144, 148-150, 152, 154-156, 184
rebirth, collective, 141
relationships, 13, 21, 37, 42, 44, 62-63, 69, 92, 99, 104, 177
Renegade, 153-154, 156, 181, 186
Rescue Dawn, 179
Return of the King, 46, 106, 129, 132, 136, 178, 182, 185-186, *see also Lord of the Rings* trilogy
Revolutionary Road, 179, 182
Ring bearer, 16, 22
ritual, 24, 100, 125-126, 128, 134, 153, 162
Road to Perdition, 82, 182
Rob Roy, 82
Robbins, Tim, 101, 137
Rodan, 28
Rodriguez, Robert, 14, 16
romantic comedy, 52, 68
Romy and Michelle's High School Reunion, 70, 182
Room with a View, 70, 182
Rosemary's Baby, 61
rottentomatoes.com, 55, 57
Safe Zone, the, 6, 35, 46, 50, 76, 78-81, 83-84, 87, 91, 93, 95, 100, 107-108, 111, 113, 130, 136, 145, 155

Saving Private Ryan, 77, 114, 182
Scarface, 109
Schindler's List, 82
Schubert, Franz, 151
Scorsese, Martin, 133
Scott, Ridley, 18, 19-21, 24, 59, 70, 104, 113-114, 120
Secret Garden, The, 135
self-empowerment, 161, 172
Se7en, 58, 182
Seventh Voyage of Sinbad, The, 28
sexuality, 117-118, 133, 151
Shadow (Jungian), 67
shamanism, 100-102, 128, 149, 153-155
shame, 42-44, 53, 66, 95, 133, 139-140, 165
Shawshank Redemption, The, 82, 97, 137-138, 182, 185
Shrek, 159
Sin City, 69, 110
slapstick, 68, 98
Slum Dog Millionaire, 179, 182
soundtracks, 82
Spacey, Kevin, 58
spaghetti Westerns, 82
Sparks, Ason, 5, 32
Sparks, Bryn, 5, 15, 17, 32-33, 54-55, 122, 137, 179
Sparks, Cary, 5, 17, 18, 20, 30, 52, 54-55, 62, 69, 70-72, 122
Squid and the Whale, The, 63, 183
Spiderman, 120
Spielberg, Steven, 93, 97, 99-100, 114
Spirited Away, 90, 183
spiritual practice, 12, 21, 25, 33, 141
Springsteen, Bruce, 13
Star Trek, the Next Generation, 142
Star Wars, 27-28, 59, 79, 96, 98, 118, 132, 154, 183, 185
Stardust, 179
Stewart, Patrick, 142
Stoltz, Eric, 115
Stone, Oliver, 114
Sullivan, Ed, 103
Sunshine, 6, 142, 179-180
Supreme Ordeal, 110-111, 128, 130, 136, 154
surrender, 29, 50, 90, 135, 144, 148-149, 151
Sutherland, Donald, 63

INDEX

synchronicity, 150
Syriana, 89
Tarantino, Quentin, 88, 115
Taris Bulbar, 28
Terminator, 65, 69, 144, 183
Terms of Endearment, 98-99, 183
therapy, 14, 16, 26, 28, 33, 35, 42, 58, 61, 63-65, 111, 138, 168, 171-172, 175
There Will Be Blood, 179
Thief, 112, 183
Thin Red Line, The, 46, 69,82, 88, 91-92, 114, 132, 183-184
Thurman, Uma, 115
Titanic, 82, 84, 142
tomatometer, 55, 57
toxic womb, 79, 91, 93, 95-96, 156
Toy Story, 159
trailers, 56
Training Day, 34, 183
Trainspotting, 84
transformation, 12-15, 24, 26, 33, 35-36, 46-47, 58, 62, 76-77, 79, 101, 106, 111, 126-127, 145, 147, 160, 162, 172-174, 176
Trapped Zone, the, 6, 35, 46, 50, 76, 80, 87, 94-108, 110-111, 115-116, 123, 130, 139, 173
trauma, 63, 91, 156, 171-172
Travolta, John, 115
tunnel, 50, 80, 95, 104-108, 110-111, 123, 130, 132, 137, 143, 173
, as archetype, 106
Twenty Thousand Leagues Under the Sea, 27, 43, 84
Tyler Moore, Mary, 63
Tyrell, Elden, 124, 173
unconscious, the, 36, 37, 40, 67-68, 102, 118, 126, 174
underworld, 100-101, 103
vampire movies, 52, 59, 118-119
Vangelis, 19, 21
victimization, 58, 67, 107-108, 111, 160, 169
Vietnam war, 101, 124
violence, 66-68, 70, 110, 119, 133, 151
Vipassana, 162
War Zone, the, 6, 35, 46, 50, 76, 80, 87, 109-128, 130-131, 133, 141, 145
Warrior, 80, 120

Washington, Denzel, 34
Weaver, Sigourney, 119
Weir, Peter, 65
Who, The, 138
Williams, John, 93
Winger, Debra, 98
Wizard of Oz, The, 183
Wolf Creek, 58, 183
womb, 19, 48, 76, 79, 83, 86-88, 92, 95, 97-98, 103, 107, 113, 156, 168
womb, good, 48, 79, 81, 83, 87, 91, 93, 97-98, 107, 113
womb, toxic, 80
World Tree, the, 101
World War II, 77, 88
yoga, movies as a, 4, 12, 14, 16, 21-22, 29, 34-35, 56, 65, 69, 98, 132, 141, 168, 175, 177
Zimmer, Hans, 91

Tav Sparks is an author, international workshop leader, and owner and Director of Grof Transpersonal Training, a program which offers certification in Holotropic Breathwork™. He lives in Mill Valley, California, with his wife, Cary, and son, Bryn. His son, Ason, and his grandsons, Dallin and Kellin, live in Georgia. For more about Tav Sparks, Movie Yoga, and Holotropic Breathwork:

www.tavsparks.com
www.movieyoga.com
www.holotropic.com

photo by Gordon Edwards

Other Books by Tav Sparks

The Wide Open Door: The Twelve Steps, Spiritual Tradition & the New Psychology by Tav Sparks. This book connects The Twelve Steps of Alcoholics Anonymous to some of the world's greatest spiritual philosophies. The book invites us to rediscover the Source behind the Steps through direct personal experience within ourselves and with our Higher Power and discusses the experiences of surrender, death and rebirth, and wholeness, especially in doing Eleventh Step work.

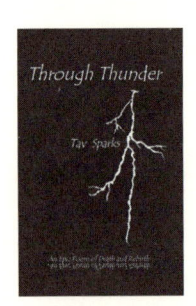

Through Thunder: An Epic Poem of Death and Rebirth by Tav Sparks. In the midst of his stormy years and dark night of the soul, twenty some years ago, Tav Sparks spontaneously wrote this "epic" poem. *Through Thunder* feels and sounds us through the archetypal "Hero's Journey" described by Joseph Campbell. It draws the perennial, turbulent, death-rebirth map of psychospiritual awakening, a process experienced by the mystics of all religions.

Hanford Mead Pubishers, Inc.
www.hanfordmead.com